LUDWIG WITTGENSTEIN
A MEMOIR

LUDWIG WITTGENSTEIN

LUDWIG WITTGENSTEIN
A MEMOIR

By NORMAN MALCOLM
Professor of Philosophy, Cornell University

With a Biographical Sketch by
GEORG HENRIK VON WRIGHT
Professor of Philosophy in the University of Helsingfors

OXFORD UNIVERSITY PRESS
LONDON   OXFORD   NEW YORK

First published by Oxford University Press, London, 1958
First issued as an Oxford University Press paperback, 1962
This reprint 1978
Printed in the United States of America

OXFORD UNIVERSITY PRESS
Oxford   London   Glasgow
New York   Toronto   Melbourne   Wellington
Ibadan   Nairobi   Dar es Salaam   Cape Town
Kuala Lumpur   Singapore   Jakarta   Hong Kong   Tokyo
Delhi   Bombay   Calcutta   Madras   Karachi

CONTENTS

NOTE

The Biographical Sketch by Georg Henrik von Wright was first published, in Swedish, in the year-book *Ajatus* of the Philosophical Society of Finland, in 1954. An English translation appeared in the *Philosophical Review*, published by Cornell University Press, in 1955. The Biographical Sketch was published along with Norman Malcolm's *Memoir*, by OXFORD UNIVERSITY PRESS in 1958. The Sketch was extensively revised by Professor von Wright for the present edition.

BIOGRAPHICAL SKETCH

by Georg Henrik von Wright

❖

On 29 April 1951 there died at Cambridge, England, one of the greatest and most influential philosophers of our time, Ludwig Wittgenstein.

It has been said that Wittgenstein inspired two important schools of thought, both of which he repudiated. The one is so-called logical positivism or logical empiricism, which played a prominent role during the decade immediately preceding the Second World War. The other is an even more heterogeneous trend which cannot be covered by *one* name. In its early phase it was sometimes called the Cambridge School of analysis. After the war its influence came to prevail at Oxford and the movement became known as linguistic philosophy or the Oxford School.

It is true that the philosophy of Wittgenstein has been of great importance to both of these trends in contemporary thought: to the first, his early work *Tractatus Logico-Philosophicus* and discussions with some members of the Vienna Circle; to the second, besides the *Tractatus*, his lectures at Cambridge and also glimpses of the works which he did not publish in his lifetime. It is also partly true that Wittgenstein repudiated the results of his own influence. He did not participate in the world wide discussion to which his work and thought had given rise. He was of the opinion—justified, I believe—that his ideas were usually misunderstood and distorted even by those who professed to be his disciples. He doubted that he would be better understood in the future. He once said that he felt as

1

though he were writing for people who would think in a quite different way, breathe a different air of life, from that of present-day men. For people of a different culture, as it were.[1] That was *one* reason why he did not himself publish his later works.

Wittgenstein avoided publicity. He withdrew from every contact with his surroundings which he thought undesirable. Outside the circle of his family and personal friends, very little was known about his life and character. His inaccessibility contributed to absurd legends about his personality and to widespread misunderstandings of his teaching. The data published in his obituaries have often been erroneous and the atmosphere of most biographical articles on Wittgenstein which I have read has been alien to their subject.

Ludwig Josef Johann Wittgenstein was born in Vienna on 26 April 1889. The Wittgenstein family had migrated from Saxony to Austria. It is of Jewish descent. It is not, contrary to what has often been stated, related to the house of princes of the same name. Wittgenstein's grandfather was a convert from the Jewish religion to Protestantism. His mother was a Roman Catholic. Ludwig Wittgenstein was baptized in the Catholic Church.

Wittgenstein's father must have been a man of remarkable intelligence and will-power. He was an engineer who became a leading figure in the steel and iron industry of the Danubean Monarchy. Wittgenstein's mother was responsible for a strong artistic influence in the family. Both she and her husband were highly musical. The wealthy and cultured home of the Wittgensteins became a centre of musical life. Johannes Brahms was a close friend of the family.

Ludwig was the youngest of five brothers and three sisters. Nature was lavish to all the children both in respect of character

[1] See the Preface to *Philosophische Bemerkungen* (1964).

and of artistic and intellectual talents. Ludwig Wittgenstein was undoubtedly a most uncommon man. Though he was free from that form of vanity which shows itself in a desire to seem different, it was inevitable that he should stand out sharply from his surroundings. It is probably true that he lived on the border of mental illness. A fear of being driven across it followed him throughout his life. But it would be wrong to say of his work that it had a morbid character. It is deeply original but not at all eccentric. It has the same naturalness, frankness, and freedom from all artificiality that was characteristic of him.

Wittgenstein was educated at home until he was fourteen. For three years thereafter he was at a school at Linz in Upper Austria. It seems to have been his wish to study physics with Boltzmann in Vienna. However, Boltzmann died in 1906, the same year that Wittgenstein finished school. Wittgenstein proceeded to the Technische Hochschule in Berlin-Charlottenburg.

That he chose to study engineering was a consequence of his early interests and talents, rather than of his father's influence. Throughout his life he was extremely interested in machinery. While a small boy he constructed a sewing machine that aroused much admiration. Even in his last years he could spend a whole day with his beloved steam-engines in the South Kensington Museum. There are several anecdotes of his serving as a mechanic when some machinery got out of order.

Wittgenstein remained in Berlin until the spring of 1908. Then he went to England. In the summer of 1908 he was experimenting with kites at The Kite Flying Upper Atmosphere Station near Glossop, in Derbyshire. The same autumn he registered as a research student in the department of engineering at the University of Manchester. He was registered there until the autumn of 1911, but spent substantial periods on the continent. During those three years he was occupied with research in aeronautics. From his kite-flying experiments he passed on to the construction of a jet reaction propeller for aircraft. At first it was the engine that absorbed his interest, but soon he concentrated on the design of the propeller, which was essentially a mathematical task. It was from this time that Wittgenstein's interests began to shift, first to pure mathematics and then to the foundations of mathematics.

Wittgenstein once mentioned to me that the problems on which he worked during his Manchester years have since become very urgent. I regret that I was not curious enough to ask him more. I assume that he was thinking of the role which the reaction engine has come to play, especially in aeronautics.[1]

In Wittgenstein's life the years from 1906 to 1912 were a time of painful seeking and of final awakening to clarity about his vocation. He told me that in those years he was constantly unhappy. To his restlessness bear witness the several interruptions of work already begun and the flights to something new: the departure from Germany to England, the experiments with kites, the construction of the jet engine, the design of the propeller, the interest in pure mathematics and finally in the philosophy of mathematics.

It is said that Wittgenstein asked someone for advice about literature on the foundations of mathematics and was directed to Bertrand Russell's *Principles of Mathematics*, which had appeared in 1903. It seems clear that this book profoundly affected Wittgenstein's development. It was probably it which led him to study the works of Frege. The 'new' logic, which in

[1] Data about Wittgenstein's time at Manchester have been recorded by Mr. W. Eccles and Mr. W. Mays. The design of the reaction engine and a number of other documents relating to this period in Wittgenstein's life have been deposited in the University Library at Manchester. I am told that Wittgenstein had patented some of his inventions in the field of aeronautics.

Frege and Russell had two of its most brilliant representatives, became the gateway through which Wittgenstein entered philosophy.

If I remember rightly,[1] Wittgenstein told me that he had read Schopenhauer's *Die Welt als Wille und Vorstellung* in his youth and that his first philosophy was a Schopenhauerian epistemological idealism. Of how this interest was related to his interest in logic and the philosophy of mathematics I know nothing, except that I remember his saying that it was Frege's conceptual realism which made him abandon his earlier idealistic views.

Having decided to give up his studies in engineering, Wittgenstein first went to Jena in Germany to discuss his plans with Frege. It was apparently Frege who advised Wittgenstein to go to Cambridge and study with Russell. He followed the advice.[2]

This was probably in the autumn of 1911.[3] At the beginning of the following year he was admitted to Trinity College and registered in the University, first as an undergraduate and later as an 'advanced student'. He was at Cambridge for all three terms of the year 1912 and the first two terms of 1913. At the beginning of the autumn of 1913 he visited Norway with David Pinsent, a young mathematician with whom he had made

[1] The biographical information which I acquired from conversations with Wittgenstein I did not record on paper until after his death. I felt very strongly that it would have been improper to write them down following our conversations. He did not often talk about his past and only rarely of his youth, which was to him a painful recollection. The idea that someone was collecting data for a biography would certainly have been deeply distasteful to him.

[2] This is how Wittgenstein related the matter to me. His account is confirmed by notes made by his sister Hermine. Russell seems, therefore, to be mistaken when in his memorial article in *Mind*, n.s., LX (1951), he says that Wittgenstein had not known Frege before he came to Cambridge.

[3] I have not been able to fix the exact dates of Wittgenstein's first visit to Frege and arrival at Cambridge. He was registered at Manchester for the Michaelmas term of 1911.

friends at Cambridge. After a short visit to England in October, he returned to Norway alone and took up residence on a farm at Skjolden in Sogn north-east of Bergen. Here he lived for most of the time until the outbreak of the war in 1914. He liked the people and the country very much. Eventually he learned to speak Norwegian fairly well. In an isolated place near Skjolden he built himself a hut, where he could live in complete seclusion.

The decade before the first Great War was a period of exceptional intellectual activity at Cambridge. Bertrand Russell had arrived at the summit of his powers. He and A. N. White-head wrote *Principia Mathematica,* a milestone in the history of logic. The most influential philosopher was G. E. Moore. Wittgenstein soon became intimate with Russell,[1] and he saw much of Moore and Whitehead. Among Wittgenstein's friends during his early years at Cambridge should also be mentioned J. M. Keynes, the economist, G. H. Hardy, the mathematician, and the logician W. E. Johnson. Wittgenstein's *Tractatus* is dedicated to the memory of David Pinsent, who fell in the war.

Beside philosophy Wittgenstein did some experimental work in psychology at Cambridge. He carried out an investigation concerning rhythm in music, at the psychological laboratory. He had hoped that the experiments would throw light on some questions of aesthetics that interested him. Wittgenstein was exceptionally musical, even if one judged by the highest standards. He played the clarinet, and for a time he wished to become a conductor. He had a rare talent for whistling. It was a great pleasure to hear him whistle through a whole concerto, interrupting himself only to draw the listener's attention to some detail of the musical texture.

An important source of our knowledge of Wittgenstein dur-

[1] Russell says, in the memorial article referred to, 'Getting to know Wittgenstein was one of the most exciting intellectual adventures of my life'.

ing these years is a series of his letters to Russell. Another is
Pinsent's diary of their Cambridge life and their travels to
Iceland and Norway. The letters and the diary help to illuminate Wittgenstein's personality, not only as a young man, but
also as he appeared to his friends of the 1930's and 1940's. The
letters also contain interesting information about the gradual
development of the work which first established Wittgenstein's
fame as a philosopher.

Wittgenstein's earliest philosophical investigations were in the
realm of the problems with which Frege and Russell had dealt.
Concepts such as 'propositional function', 'variable', 'generality',
and 'identity' occupied his thoughts. He soon made an interesting discovery, a new symbolism for so-called 'truth-functions'
that led to the explanation of logical truth as 'tautology'.[1]

The oldest parts of the *Tractatus* are those dealing with logic.
Wittgenstein had formed his principal thoughts on these
matters before the outbreak of the war in 1914, and thus before
his twenty-sixth year. Later he became engrossed in a new
problem. It was the question of the nature of the significant
proposition.[2] There is a story of how the idea of language as
a picture of reality occurred to Wittgenstein.[3] It was in the
autumn of 1914, on the East front. Wittgenstein was reading
in a magazine about a law-suit in Paris concerning an automobile accident. At the trial a miniature model of the accident

[1] The symbolism in question is much the same as that explained in *Tractatus*
6.1203. The now familiar truth-tables (*Tractatus* 4.31, etc.) he invented later.

[2] 'My *whole* task consists in explaining the nature of the proposition', he
wrote in one of the philosophical notebooks that he kept during the war.

[3] There exist several, somewhat different versions of it. The story as told here
is based on an entry in Wittgenstein's philosophical notebooks in June 1930.—
It would be interesting to know whether Wittgenstein's conception of the
proposition as a picture is connected in any way with the Introduction to
Heinrich Hertz's *Die Prinzipen der Mechanik*. Wittgenstein knew this work and
held it in high esteem. There are traces of the impression that it made on him
both in the *Tractatus* and in his later writings.

was presented before the court. The model here served as a proposition; that is, as a description of a possible state of affairs. It had this function owing to a correspondence between the parts of the model (the miniature-houses, -cars, -people) and things (houses, cars, people) in reality. It now occurred to Wittgenstein that one might reverse the analogy and say that a *proposition* serves as a model or *picture*, by virtue of a similar correspondence between *its* parts and the world. The way in which the parts of the proposition are combined—the *structure* of the proposition—depicts a possible combination of elements in reality, a possible state of affairs.

Wittgenstein's *Tractatus* may be called a synthesis of the theory of truth-functions and the idea that language is a picture of reality. Out of this synthesis arises a third main ingredient of the book, its doctrine of that which cannot be *said*, only *shown*.

At the outbreak of the war, Wittgenstein entered the Austrian army as a volunteer, although he had been exempted from service because of a rupture. He served first on a vessel on the Vistula and later in an artillery workshop at Cracow. In 1915 he was ordered to Olmütz, in Moravia, to be trained as an officer. Later he fought on the East front. In 1918 he was transferred to the South front. Upon the collapse of the Austro-Hungarian army in October, he was taken prisoner by the Italians. It was not until August of the following year that he could return to Austria. During the major part of his captivity, he was in a prison camp near Monte Cassino in south Italy.

When Wittgenstein was captured he had in his rucksack the manuscript of his *Logisch-philosophische Abhandlung*, which is generally known by the Latin title proposed for it by G. E. Moore, *Tractatus Logico-Philosophicus*. He had completed the work when on a leave of absence, in August 1918. While still in captivity he got in touch with Russell by letter and was able to send the manuscript to him, thanks to the aid of one of his friends of the Cambridge years, Keynes. He also sent Frege a copy and corresponded with him.

It was Wittgenstein's habit to write down his thoughts in notebooks. The entries are usually dated, thus they compose a sort of diary. The contents of an earlier notebook are often worked over again in a later one. Sometimes he dictated to colleagues and pupils. In the spring of 1914 he dictated some thoughts on logic to Moore in Norway. In the late 20's and early 30's he dictated to Schlick and Waismann. The so-called Blue Book was dictated in conjunction with lectures at Cambridge in the academic year 1933-4. The so-called Brown Book was dictated privately to some pupils in 1934-5.[1]

Some of the notebooks which led up to the *Tractatus* have been preserved.[2] These sketches and fragments of earlier versions are of great interest, partly because they show the development of his thoughts, partly because they illuminate many difficult passages in the extremely compressed final version. I have been especially impressed by a notebook of the year 1916. It deals chiefly with the ego, the freedom of the will, the meaning of life, and death. Thus the somewhat aphoristic remarks on these topics in the *Tractatus* are sifted from a quantity of material. The notes show how strong were the impressions that Wittgenstein had received from Schopenhauer. An occasional Spinozistic flavour is also recognizable.

In the earliest notebooks a considerable part of the content is written in a code. Wittgenstein continued to use this code throughout his life. The notes in code are for the most part of a personal nature.

The period of the war was a crisis in Wittgenstein's life. To

---

[1] These two books were published in 1958 under the title *Preliminary Studies for the 'Philosophical Investigations', Generally known as The Blue and Brown Books*.
[2] Published in 1961 under the title *Notebooks 1914-1916*.

what extent the turmoil of the time and his experiences in war and captivity contributed to the crisis, I cannot say. A circumstance of great importance was that he became acquainted with the ethical and religious writings of Tolstoy. Tolstoy exercised a strong influence on Wittgenstein's view of life, and also led him to study the Gospels.

After the death of his father in 1912 Wittgenstein was in possession of a great fortune. One of his first steps after his return from the war was to give away all his money.[1] Henceforth a great simplicity, at times even an extreme frugality, became characteristic of his life. His dress was unconventional; it is impossible to imagine him with necktie or hat. A bed, a table, and a few deck-chairs were all of his furniture. Ornamental objects of whatever kind were banished from his surroundings.

After the war Wittgenstein took up the vocation of schoolmaster. In 1919–20 he was trained at a college for teachers in elementary schools (*Lehrerbildungsanstalt*) in Vienna. From 1920 to 1926 he taught in various remote villages in the districts of Schneeberg and Semmering in Lower Austria. This suited his wish for a simple and secluded life. In other ways it did not suit him well. It appears that he was in constant friction with the people around him. Finally there was a serious crisis. Wittgenstein resigned his post and quitted for ever the career of schoolmaster. He went to work as a gardener's assistant with the monks at Hütteldorf, near Vienna.

In this period, Wittgenstein contemplated entering a monas-

[1] Before the war Wittgenstein had made a large anonymous grant for the promotion of literature. Two poets of whom he was in this manner a benefactor were Georg Trakl and Rainer Maria Rilke. (For more details see Ludwig Ficker's article 'Rilke und der unbekannte Freund' in *Der Brenner*, 1954.) It may be remarked in passing that Wittgenstein had a high opinion of Trakl's talent, but that later in life, at least, he did not greatly admire Rilke, whose poetry he thought artificial.

tery. The same thought occurred to him at other times in his life too. That it never came true was, partly at least, because for him the inner conditions of monastic life were not satisfied.

His service with the monks soon came to an end. In the autumn of 1926 Wittgenstein accepted a task that absorbed his time and his genius for two years. He built a mansion in Vienna for one of his sisters. In the beginning he co-operated with his friend, the architect Paul Engelmann. But soon Wittgenstein took over alone. The building is his work down to the smallest detail and is highly characteristic of its creator. It is free from all decoration and marked by a severe exactitude in measure and proportion. Its beauty is of the same simple and static kind that belongs to the sentences of the *Tractatus*. It does not seem to me that the building can be classified as belonging to some one style. But the horizontal roofs and the materials—concrete, glass, and steel—remind the spectator of typically 'modern' architecture. (In 1914 Wittgenstein had come to know Adolf Loos, whose work he respected.)

During this same time Wittgenstein did a sculpture in the studio of his friend, the sculptor Drobil. It is the head of a young woman. The features have the same finished and restful beauty one finds in Greek sculptures of the classical period and which seems to have been Wittgenstein's ideal. In general, there is a striking contrast between the restlessness, the continual searching and changing, in Wittgenstein's life and personality, and the perfection and elegance of his finished work.

The author of the *Tractatus* thought he had solved all philosophical problems. It was consistent with this view that he should give up philosophy. The publication of the book was largely due to Russell. In 1919 the two friends met in Holland to discuss the manuscript. The problem of finding a publisher caused difficulties and the matter was further complicated by Wittgenstein's strong disapproval of Russell's introduction to the book. In July 1920 Wittgenstein wrote to Russell that he himself would take no further steps to have it published and that Russell could do with it as he wished. The German text was published in 1921 in the last issue of Ostwald's *Annalen der Naturphilosophie*. In the following year it was published in London with a parallel English translation. The translation contains a number of errors which corrupt the meaning.[1] A new translation was published in 1961.

During his years as schoolmaster and architect, Wittgenstein was not completely cut off from contact with the philosophical world. In 1923 a young man from Cambridge, Frank Ramsey, visited him at Puchberg. Ramsey had assisted in the translation of the *Tractatus* and had written, at the age of twenty, a remarkably penetrating review of the book for *Mind*. The visit was repeated a year later. Ramsey tried to persuade Wittgenstein to come to England on a visit. He was helped in his efforts by Keynes, who even procured money for the purpose. In the summer of 1925 Wittgenstein finally did visit his English friends.

After Ramsey, Moritz Schlick, a professor in Vienna, managed to establish contact with Wittgenstein. The study of the latter's book had made a deep impression on this honest and intelligent man, who was to become famous as the founder and leader of the Vienna Circle. Wittgenstein's influence on the philosophic movement which the Vienna Circle started is thus in part due to a personal connexion, lasting for a number of years, between Wittgenstein and Schlick. Another member of the Circle who was personally strongly influenced by Wittgenstein was Friedrich Waismann.

Wittgenstein said that he returned to philosophy because he

---

[1] The translator's note, according to which 'the proofs of the translation ... have been very carefully revised by the author himself', does not agree with what Wittgenstein later told several of his friends.

felt that he could again do creative work. An external circumstance of this important step may have been that in March of 1928 he had heard Brouwer lecture in Vienna on the foundations of mathematics. (It is rumoured to have been this which stirred him to take up philosophy again.) Early in 1929 Wittgenstein arrived at Cambridge. He was first registered as a research student, a somewhat unusual status for a man whom many already regarded as one of the foremost living representatives of his subject. The idea was that he should work for the Ph.D. It turned out, however, that he could count his pre-war residence at Cambridge as credit towards the degree and could present his book, published eight years earlier, as a thesis. He received his degree in June 1929. The following year he was made a Fellow of Trinity College.

Soon after his return to Cambridge Wittgenstein began to write down philosophical thoughts. His output in the years 1929–1932 was, as always from then on, tremendous. From the notebooks in handwriting he sifted remarks for two bulky typescripts. One is called *Philosophische Bemerkungen*; for the other he contemplated the names 'Philosophische Betrachtungen' or 'Philosophische Grammatik'. They are virtually completed works.[1] But Wittgenstein did not publish them.

The only philosophical writing that Wittgenstein himself published subsequent to the *Tractatus* was the paper 'Some

[1] It was in reference to *Philosophische Bemerkungen* that Bertrand Russell, in 1930, reported to the Council of Trinity College, which was considering the award of a grant to Wittgenstein, as follows: 'The theories contained in this new work of Wittgenstein are novel, very original, and indubitably important. Whether they are true, I do not know. As a logician, who likes simplicity, I should wish to think that they are not, but from what I have read of them I am quite sure that he ought to have an opportunity to work them out, since when completed they may easily prove to constitute a whole new philosophy.' (Quoted with the permission of Lord Russell and the Council of Trinity College, Cambridge.)

Remarks on Logical Form'.[1] This paper was supposed to have
been read by him to the annual meeting of British philosophers
—the Joint Session of the Mind Association and the Aristotelian Society—in 1929. The papers prepared for these meetings
are printed and distributed to the participants in advance, and
are subsequently collected in a Supplementary Volume to the
Proceedings of the Aristotelian Society. Wittgenstein surprised his audience by talking to them on an entirely different
topic—the notion of the infinite in mathematics—and not reading his paper at all. Wittgenstein himself thought this paper
worthless.

Wittgenstein's writings of the period anterior to the Blue
Book are of considerable interest, not least to the historian of
philosophic ideas. Their intrinsic value is, I think, less than
that of either the *Tractatus* or the *Investigations*. This is natural,
considering that they represent a transitional stage in Wittgenstein's development.

It will probably remain a matter of future debate to what
extent there is continuity between the 'early' Wittgenstein of the
Tractatus and the 'later' Wittgenstein of the *Investigations*. The
writings from 1929 to 1932 testify to a continuous development
and struggle—out of the former work and in the direction of
the later. The Blue Book of 1933–1934 conveys more the
impression of a first, still somewhat rough version of a radically
new philosophy. I myself find it difficult to fit the Blue Book
into the development of Wittgenstein's thoughts. The Brown
Book is a somewhat different case. It may be regarded as a
preliminary version of the beginning of the *Investigations*. In
August 1936 Wittgenstein began a revision, in German, of the
Brown Book which had been dictated in English one year

[1] While he was a schoolmaster he published a German glossary for elementary schools, *Wörterbuch für Volks- und Bürgerschulen* (Holder-Piehler-Tempski,
Vienna, 1926).

earlier. He called the revision *Philosophische Untersuchungen*. He soon abandoned work on it as unsatisfactory, and made a fresh start in the autumn of the same year. What he then wrote is substantially identical with the first 189 sections of the *Investigations* in its printed form.

The young Wittgenstein had learned from Frege and Russell. His problems were in part theirs. The later Wittgenstein, I should say, has no ancestors in the history of thought. His work signalizes a radical departure from previously existing paths of philosophy. But his problems grew to a great extent out of the *Tractatus*. This, I think, is the reason why Wittgenstein wanted the work which embodied his new philosophy to be printed together with the work of his youth.[1]

It is sometimes said that the later Wittgenstein resembles Moore. This is hardly true. Moore's and Wittgenstein's ways of thinking are in fact utterly different. Although their friendship lasted until the latter's death, I do not believe that there is any trace of an influence of Moore's philosophy on Wittgenstein. What Wittgenstein appreciated was Moore's intellectual vitality, his love of truth and freedom from vanity.

Of great importance in the origination of Wittgenstein's new ideas was the criticism to which his earlier views were subjected by two of his friends. One was Ramsey, whose premature death in 1930 was a heavy loss to contemporary thought. The other was Piero Sraffa, an Italian economist who had come to Cambridge shortly before Wittgenstein returned there. It was above all Sraffa's acute and forceful criticism that compelled Wittgenstein to abandon his earlier views and set out upon new roads. He said that his discussions with Sraffa made him feel like a tree from which all branches had been cut. That this tree could become green again was due to its own vitality. The later Wittgenstein did not receive an inspiration from outside

[1] See the Preface to *Philosophische Untersuchungen*.

Ludwig Wittgenstein

like that which the earlier Wittgenstein got from Frege and Russell.

From 1929 until his death, Wittgenstein lived—with some interruptions—in England. He became a British subject when, after the 'Anschluss', he would have had to give up his Austrian passport, and the choice for him was between German and British nationality. But in general he was not fond of English ways of life and he disliked the academic atmosphere of Cambridge. When his Fellowship at Trinity College expired in 1935,[1] he had plans for settling in the Soviet Union. He visited the country with a friend and apparently was pleased with the visit. That nothing came of his plans was due, partly at least, to the harshening of conditions in Russia in the middle 30's. So Wittgenstein remained at Cambridge until the end of the academic year 1935–6. Thereafter he lived for nearly a year in his hut in Norway. It was then that he began to write the *Philosophical Investigations*. In 1937 he returned to Cambridge, where, two years later, he succeeded Moore to the chair in philosophy.

From the beginning of 1930, with some interruptions, Wittgenstein lectured at Cambridge. As might be expected, his lectures were highly 'unacademic'.[2] He nearly always held them in his own room or in the college rooms of a friend. He had no manuscript or notes. He *thought* before the class. The impression was of a tremendous concentration. The exposition usually led to a question, to which the audience were supposed to suggest an answer. The answers in turn became starting points for new thoughts leading to new questions. It depended

[1] The Fellowship was prolonged to include the whole of the academic year 1935–6. When he became a professor, Wittgenstein was again made a Fellow of Trinity College.

[2] A vivid and true impression of Wittgenstein as a teacher is conveyed by the memorial article, signed D. A. T. G. – A. C. J., in *The Australasian Journal of Philosophy*, XXIX (1951).

on the audience, to a great extent, whether the discussion became fruitful and whether the connecting thread was kept in sight from beginning to end of a lecture and from one lecture to another. Many of his audience were highly qualified people in their various fields. Moore attended Wittgenstein's lectures for some years in the early 30's.[1] Several of those who later became leading philosophers in England, the United States, or Australia heard Wittgenstein lecture at Cambridge. There exist good, more or less verbatim notes of some of his lecture courses.

Before Wittgenstein assumed his chair, the Second Great War broke out. I think one may say that he wished for the war. But, as in 1914, he did not want to watch it from an ivory tower. For some time he served as a porter at Guy's Hospital in London. Later he worked in a medical laboratory at Newcastle. It should be mentioned that Wittgenstein had been strongly attracted to the medical profession and that once in the 30's he seriously considered leaving philosophy to take up medicine. During his time at Newcastle he devised some technical innovations that proved useful.

It need not surprise us that Wittgenstein's restless genius was not happy in academic routine. It is likely that if the war had not come his tenure of the chair would have been even more brief. In the Easter term of 1947 he gave his last lectures at Cambridge. In the autumn he was away on a leave, and from the end of the year he ceased to be a professor. He wanted to devote all his remaining strength to his research. As so often before in his life, he went to live in seclusion. For the winter of 1948 he settled on a farm in the Irish countryside. After that he

---

[1] Moore has published a full account and an interesting discussion of these lectures in *Mind*, n.s., LXIII–LXIV (1954–5). Moore's articles can be said to be a commentary on some of the views which Wittgenstein held in the 'period of transition' (1929–33) preceding the Blue Book.

lived quite by himself in a hut beside the ocean, in Galway on the Irish west coast. His neighbours were primitive fishermen. It is said that Wittgenstein became a legend among his neighbours because he had tamed so many birds; they used to come every day to be fed by him. The life in Galway, however, became physically too strenuous for him, and in the autumn of 1948 he moved to a hotel in Dublin. From then until early spring of the following year he had an excellent working period. It was then he completed the second part of the *Philosophical Investigations*.

During the last two years of his life Wittgenstein was severely ill. In the autumn of 1949 it was found that he suffered from cancer. Wittgenstein was then on a visit to Cambridge after his return from a short stay in the United States. He did not go back to Ireland, but remained with friends in Oxford and in Cambridge. In the autumn of 1950 he visited Norway with a friend and even had plans of settling there again at the beginning of the following year. During part of his illness he was incapable of work. But it is remarkable that during the last two months he was not in bed and was apparently in the best of spirits. As late as two days before his death he wrote down thoughts that are equal to the best he produced.

Wittgenstein's very unusual and forceful personality exerted a great influence over others. No one who came in touch with him could fail to be impressed. Some were repelled. Most were attracted or fascinated. One can say that Wittgenstein avoided making acquaintances, but needed and sought friendships. He was an incomparable, but demanding, friend. I believe that most of those who loved him and had his friendship also feared him.

Just as there were many groundless legends concerning Wittgenstein's life and personality, so there grew up much unsound sectarianism among his pupils. This caused Wittgenstein much pain. He thought that his influence as a teacher was, on the whole, harmful to the development of independent minds in his disciples. I am afraid that he was right. And I believe that I can partly understand why it should be so. Because of the depth and originality of his thinking, it is very difficult to understand Wittgenstein's ideas and even more difficult to incorporate them into one's own thinking. At the same time the magic of his personality and style was most inviting and persuasive. To learn from Wittgenstein without coming to adopt his forms of expression and catch-words and even to imitate his tone of voice, his mien and gestures, was almost impossible. The danger was that the thoughts should deteriorate into a jargon. The teaching of great men often has a simplicity and naturalness which makes the difficult appear easy to grasp. Their disciples usually become, therefore, insignificant epigones. The historic significance of such men does not manifest itself in their disciples but through influences of a more indirect, subtle and, often, unexpected kind.

Wittgenstein's most characteristic features were his great and pure seriousness and powerful intelligence. I have never met a man who impressed me so strongly in either respect.

It seems to me that there are two forms of seriousness of character. One is fixed in 'strong principles'; the other springs from a passionate heart. The former has to do with morality and the latter, I believe, is closer to religion. Wittgenstein was acutely and even painfully sensitive to considerations of duty, but the earnestness and severity of his personality were more of the second kind. Yet I do not know whether he can be said to have been 'religious' in any but a trivial sense of the word. Certainly he did not have a Christian faith. But neither was his view of life un-Christian, pagan, as was Goethe's. To say that Wittgenstein was not a pantheist is to say something important. 'God does not reveal himself *in* the world', he wrote in the *Tractatus*. The thought of God, he said, was above all for him the thought of the fearful judge.

Wittgenstein had the conviction, he sometimes said, that he was doomed. His outlook was typically one of gloom. Modern times were to him a dark age.[1] His idea of the helplessness of human beings was not unlike certain doctrines of predestination.

Wittgenstein was not, strictly speaking, a learned man. His temperament was very different from that of the typical scholar. 'Cool objectivity' and 'detached meditation' are labels which do not suit him at all. He put his whole soul into everything he did. His life was a constant journey, and doubt was the moving force within him. He seldom looked back on his earlier positions, and when he did so it was usually to repudiate them.

Knowledge, for Wittgenstein, was intimately connected with doing. It is significant that his first studies were in the technical sciences. He had a knowledge of mathematics and physics not derived from extensive reading, but from a working familiarity with mathematical and experimental techniques. His many artistic interests had the same active and living character. He could design a house, make a sculpture, or conduct an orchestra. Perhaps he would never have achieved mastery in those fields. But he was no 'dilettante'. Every manifestation of his multi-dimensional spirit came from the same earnest drive to create.

Wittgenstein had done no systematic reading in the classics of philosophy. He could read only what he could wholeheartedly assimilate. We have seen that as a young man he read Schopenhauer. From Spinoza, Hume and Kant he said that he could get only occasional glimpses of understanding. I do not think that he could have enjoyed Aristotle or Leibniz, two great logicians before him. But it is significant that he did read

[1] See the Preface to *Philosophical Investigations*: 'the darkness of these times'.

and enjoy Plato. He must have recognized congenial features, both in Plato's literary and philosophic method and in the temperament behind the thoughts.

Wittgenstein received deeper impressions from some writers in the borderland between philosophy, religion, and poetry than from the philosophers, in the restricted sense of the word. Among the former are St. Augustine, Kierkegaard, Dostoievsky, and Tolstoy. The philosophical sections of St. Augustine's *Confessions* show a striking resemblance to Wittgenstein's own way of doing philosophy. Between Wittgenstein and Pascal there is a trenchant parallelism which deserves closer study. It should also be mentioned that Wittgenstein held the writings of Otto Weininger in high regard.

An aspect of Wittgenstein's work which is certain to attract growing attention is its language. It would be surprising if he were not one day ranked among the classic writers of German prose. The literary merits of the *Tractatus* have not gone unnoticed. The language of the *Philosophical Investigations* is equally remarkable. The style is simple and perspicuous, the construction of sentences firm and free, the rhythm flows easily. The form is sometimes that of dialogue, with questions and replies; sometimes, as in the *Tractatus*, it condenses to aphorisms. There is a striking absence of all literary ornamentation, and of technical jargon or terminology. The union of measured moderation with richest imagination, the simultaneous impression of natural continuation and surprising turns, leads one to think of some other great productions of the genius of Vienna. (Schubert was Wittgenstein's favourite composer.)

It may appear strange that Schopenhauer, one of the masters of philosophic prose, did not influence Wittgenstein's style. An author, however, who reminds one, often astonishingly, of Wittgenstein is Lichtenberg. Wittgenstein esteemed him highly. To what extent, if any, he can be said to have learned from him I do not know. It is deserving of mention that some of Lichtenberg's thoughts on philosophic questions show a striking resemblance to Wittgenstein's.[1]

It is fairly certain that both the work and personality of Wittgenstein will provoke varying comments and different interpretations in the future. The author of the sentences 'The riddle does not exist' and 'Everything that can be said can be said clearly' was himself an enigma, and his sentences have a content that often lies deep beneath the surface of the language. In Wittgenstein many contrasts meet. It has been said that he was at once a logician and a mystic. *Neither* term is appropriate, but each hints at something true. Those who approach Wittgenstein's work will sometimes look for its essence in a rational, matter-of-fact dimension, and sometimes more in a supra-empirical, metaphysical one. In the existing literature on Wittgenstein there are examples of both conceptions. Such 'interpretations' have little significance. They must appear as falsifications to anyone who tries to understand Wittgenstein in his rich complexity. They are interesting only as showing in how many directions his influence extends. I have sometimes thought that what makes a man's work *classic* is often just this multiplicity, which invites and at the same time resists our craving for clear understanding.

[1] See my paper, 'Georg Christoph Lichtenberg als Philosoph', *Theoria*, VIII (1942).

LUDWIG WITTGENSTEIN

A MEMOIR

I FIRST saw Wittgenstein in the Michaelmas term of 1938, my first term at Cambridge. At a meeting of the Moral Science Club, after the paper for the evening was read and the discussion started, someone began to stammer a remark. He had extreme difficulty in expressing himself and his words were unintelligible to me. I whispered to my neighbour, 'Who is that?': he replied, 'Wittgenstein.' I was astonished, because, for one reason, I had expected the famous author of the *Tractatus Logico-Philosophicus* to be an elderly man, whereas this man looked *young*—perhaps about thirty-five. (His actual age was forty-nine.) His face was lean and brown, his profile was aquiline and strikingly beautiful, his head was covered with a curly mass of brown hair. I observed the respectful attention that everyone in the room paid to him. After this unsuccessful beginning he did not speak for a time but was obviously struggling with his thoughts. His look was concentrated, he made striking gestures with his hands as if he were discoursing. All the others maintained an intent and expectant silence. I witnessed this phenomenon countless times thereafter and came to regard it as entirely natural.

I attended Wittgenstein's lectures, which were on the philosophical foundations of mathematics, in the Lent term of 1939. He continued on this topic in the Easter and Michaelmas terms of 1939. I think that I understood almost nothing of the lectures, until I restudied my notes approximately ten years later. Nevertheless I was aware, as others were, that Wittgenstein was doing something important. One knew that he was fighting his way through profoundly difficult problems and that his method of attacking them was absolutely original.

His lectures were given without preparation and without notes. He told me that once he had tried to lecture from notes but was disgusted with the result; the thoughts that came out were 'stale', or, as he put it to another friend, the words looked like 'corpses' when he began to read them. In the method that he came to use his only preparation for the lecture, as he told me, was to spend a few minutes before the class met, recollecting the course that the inquiry had taken at the previous meetings. At the beginning of the lecture he would give a brief summary of this and then he would start from there, trying to advance the investigation with fresh thoughts. He told me that the only thing that made it possible for him to conduct his lecture classes in this extemporaneous way was the fact that he had done and was doing a vast amount of thinking and writing about all the problems under discussion. This is undoubtedly true; nevertheless, what occurred in these class meetings was largely *new* research.

Whether lecturing or conversing privately, Wittgenstein always spoke emphatically and with a distinctive intonation. He spoke excellent English, with the accent of an educated Englishman, although occasional Germanisms would appear in his constructions. His voice was resonant, the pitch being somewhat higher than that of the normal male voice, but not unpleasant. His words came out, not fluently, but with great force. Anyone who heard him say anything knew that here was a singular person. His face was remarkably mobile and expressive when he talked. His eyes were deep and often fierce in their expression. His whole personality was commanding, even imperial.

In contrast, his dress was as simple as possible. He always

wore light grey flannel trousers, a flannel shirt open at the throat, a woollen lumber jacket or a leather jacket. Out of doors, in wet weather, he wore a tweed cap and a tan raincoat. He nearly always walked with a light cane. One could not imagine Wittgenstein in a suit, necktie, or hat. His clothes, except the raincoat, were always extremely clean and his shoes polished. He was about five feet six inches in height and slender.

He met his class twice weekly for a two-hour meeting, from five to seven p.m. He demanded promptness and became angry if someone came in two minutes late. Before he was a professor the meetings were mainly held in the college rooms of various friends of his, and thereafter in his own rooms in Whewell's Court, Trinity College. Members of the class brought in chairs or sat on the floor. At times the jam was formidable. This was especially true of the lectures that began the Michaelmas term of 1946; for about thirty people turned up and were wedged together without an inch to spare.

Wittgenstein's rooms in Whewell's Court were austerely furnished. There was no easy chair or reading lamp. There were no ornaments, paintings, or photographs. The walls were bare. In his living-room were two canvas chairs and a plain wooden chair, and in his bedroom a canvas cot. An old-fashioned iron heating stove was in the centre of the living-room. There were some flowers in a window box, and one or two flower pots in the room. There was a metal safe in which he kept his manuscripts, and a card table on which he did his writing. The rooms were always scrupulously clean.

The chairs that members of the class brought in belonged to Trinity and were kept on the landing between lectures. If someone came late this involved a considerable disruption, because chairs already placed had to be moved to make room. One had to be brave to enter after the lecture had begun, and some would go away rather than face Wittgenstein's glare.

Wittgenstein sat in a plain wooden chair in the centre of the room. Here he carried on a visible struggle with his thoughts. He often felt that he was confused, and said so. Frequently he said things like 'I'm a fool!', 'You have a dreadful teacher!', 'I'm just too stupid today'. Sometimes he expressed a doubt that he would be able to continue the lecture, but only rarely did he give up before seven o'clock.

It is hardly correct to speak of these meetings as 'lectures', although this is what Wittgenstein called them. For one thing, he was carrying on original research in these meetings. He was thinking about certain problems in a way that he could have done had he been alone. For another thing, the meetings were largely conversation. Wittgenstein commonly directed questions at various people present and reacted to their replies. Often the meetings consisted mainly of dialogue. Sometimes, however, when he was trying to draw a thought out of himself, he would prohibit, with a peremptory motion of the hand, any questions or remarks. There were frequent and prolonged periods of silence, with only an occasional mutter from Wittgenstein, and the stillest attention from the others. During these silences, Wittgenstein was extremely tense and active. His gaze was concentrated; his face was alive; his hands made arresting movements; his expression was stern. One knew that one was in the presence of extreme seriousness, absorption, and force of intellect.

Wittgenstein's personality dominated these meetings. I doubt that anyone in the class failed to be influenced by him in some way. Few of us could keep from acquiring imitations of his mannerisms, gestures, intonations, exclamations. These imitations could easily appear ridiculous when compared with their original.

Wittgenstein was a frightening person at these classes. He was very impatient and easily angered. If someone felt an objection to what he was saying he was fiercely insistent that the objection should be stated. Once when Yorick Smythies, an old friend of Wittgenstein's, was unable to put his objection into words, Wittgenstein said to him very harshly, 'I might as well talk to this stove!' Fear of Wittgenstein helped to keep our attention at a high pitch. This was a valuable result since the problems were of extreme difficulty and Wittgenstein's methods of examining them were enormously hard to understand. I was always conscious of the mental exertion required to follow him, and two hours of it was more than I was good for.

Wittgenstein's severity was connected, I think, with his passionate love of truth. He was constantly fighting with the deepest philosophical problems. The solution of one problem led to another problem. Wittgenstein was uncompromising; he had to have *complete* understanding. He drove himself fiercely. His whole being was under a tension. No one at the lectures could fail to perceive that he strained his will, as well as his intellect, to the utmost. This was one aspect of his absolute, relentless honesty. Primarily, what made him an awesome and even terrible person, both as a teacher and in personal relationships, was his ruthless integrity, which did not spare himself or anyone else.

Wittgenstein was always exhausted by his lectures. He was also revolted by them. He felt disgusted with what he had said and with himself. Often he would rush off to a cinema immediately after the class ended. As the members of the class began to move their chairs out of the room he might look imploringly at a friend and say in a low tone, 'Could you go to a flick?' On the way to the cinema Wittgenstein would buy a bun or cold pork pie and munch it while he watched the film. He insisted on sitting in the very first row of seats, so that the screen would occupy his entire field of vision, and his mind would be turned away from the thoughts of the lecture and his feelings of revulsion. Once he whispered to me 'This is like a shower bath!' His observation of the film was not relaxed or detached. He leaned tensely forward in his seat and rarely took his eyes off the screen. He hardly ever uttered comments on the episodes of the film and did not like his companion to do so. He wished to become totally absorbed in the film no matter how trivial or artificial it was, in order to free his mind temporarily from the philosophical thoughts that tortured and exhausted him. He liked American films and detested English ones. He was inclined to think that there *could not* be a decent English film. This was connected with a great distaste he had for English culture and mental habits in general. He was fond of the film stars Carmen Miranda and Betty Hutton. Before he came to visit me in America he demanded in jest that I should introduce him to Miss Hutton.

Some have thought that Wittgenstein's lectures were only for his friends and favourites. In fact he would admit anyone to his lectures. He required, however, that they should attend continuously and for a considerable period of time. He would not allow anyone to come for only one or two meetings. To one such request he replied, 'My lectures are not for tourists.' I have known two cases in which he allowed someone to come for one term only, but he was reluctant to give such permission. This was reasonable. It kept the lectures from being invaded by numbers of the curious. And it was true that one had to attend for quite a long time (at least three terms, I should say) before one could begin to get *any* grasp of what he was doing.

It did matter to him who was in his classes. He liked to discuss philosophical questions 'with friends'. It was important to him that there should be some 'friendly faces' in his classes. He often remarked that he liked a certain 'face' and he wanted that face to be there even if the person said nothing. During World War II, when he lectured on Saturdays, an American negro soldier was a member of the class. Wittgenstein remarked more than once what a friendly and good-natured face the man had, and how sorry he was when he ceased to come. Usually more than half of those who came to his first lecture in the autumn would discontinue attendance after five or six meetings, because they found the material unintelligible or uninteresting. The ten or fifteen persons who remained were, in contrast, extremely zealous in their attendance.

A curious thing, which I observed innumerable times, was that when Wittgenstein invented an example during his lectures in order to illustrate a point, he himself would grin at the absurdity of what he had imagined. But if any member of the class were to chuckle, his expression would change to severity and he would exclaim in reproof, 'No, no; I'm serious!' The imaginary events and circumstances were so odd and so far beyond the reach of natural possibility that he himself could not help being amused; yet the intention of the example, of course, was serious. Wittgenstein could not tolerate a facetious tone in his classes, the tone that is characteristic of philosophical discussion among clever people who have no serious purpose.

It is worth noting that Wittgenstein once said that a serious and good philosophical work could be written that would consist entirely of *jokes* (without being facetious). Another time he said that a philosophical treatise might contain nothing but questions (without answers). In his own writing he made wide use of both. To give an example: 'Why can't a dog simulate pain? Is he too honest?' (*Philosophical Investigations*, § 250).

Wittgenstein got acquainted with members of his class by having them individually to tea. I received such an invitation in 1939. There was no small talk. The conversation was serious and interspersed with long silences. The only topic that I recall had to do with my future. Wittgenstein wished to persuade me to give up my plan to become a teacher of philosophy. He wondered whether I could not do some manual job instead, such as working on a ranch or farm. He had an abhorrence of academic life in general and of the life of a professional philosopher in particular. He believed that a normal human being could not be a university teacher and also an honest and serious person. Of Smythies he once said: 'He will never get a lectureship. He is too serious.' Wittgenstein could not stand the society of academic colleagues. Although a Fellow of Trinity, he did not dine in Hall. He told me that he had tried to do it (there is an anecdote to the effect that he was once reprimanded by the Vice-Master for not wearing a tie at the High Table) but was revolted by the artificiality of the conversation. He really *hated* all forms of affectation and insincerity.

Wittgenstein several times renewed the attempt to persuade me to give up philosophy as a profession. He commonly did this with other students of his.

Despite these efforts he actually made it possible for me to continue the study of philosophy at Cambridge for another six months. This came about in the following way: My funds were derived from a Harvard University fellowship that I had held for two years and which could not be renewed. In the summer of 1939 my money was gone and I was under the necessity of returning to the States. But I was eager to remain a while longer. I was excited by the ideas that were in circulation at Cambridge, and I thought that I had just begun to get a slight understanding of Wittgenstein's work, an understanding that I wished very much to improve. Once when I was with Wittgenstein I mentioned my reluctance to return to the States just then. He wanted to know all about it. He then said that he saw that I was 'charmed' by Cambridge philosophy and that it would be a pity if I went away in that condition. He meant that if I stayed and got to know more about Cambridge philosophy, then I should no longer be charmed by it—which, in his opinion, would be a good thing. He thought that *he* might be able to provide me with money sufficient to live on for the next six months. And so it turned out. He gave (not lent) me a sum in cash each month from August 1939 to January of 1940, when I had to return to the States. The total amount that he gave me during that period was in the neighbourhood of eighty pounds. He would not consider a repayment.

In 1939 Wittgenstein used to call at my rooms frequently to get me to accompany him on walks. These were usually on Midsummer Common and beyond, along the river. He usually brought bread or sugar to feed the horses on the Common. A walk with Wittgenstein was very exhausting. Whatever we talked about, he turned his mind to it with great seriousness and intensity, and it was a formidable strain on me to keep up with his thoughts. He would walk in spurts, sometimes coming to a stop while he made some emphatic remark and looking into my eyes with his piercing gaze. Then he would walk rapidly for a few yards, then slow down, then speed up or come to a halt, and so on. And this uncertain ambulation was conjoined with the most exacting conversation! The freshness and depth of Wittgenstein's thinking, no matter what the topic, was highly demanding of his companion. His remarks were never *commonplace*.

When in very good spirits he would jest in a delightful manner. This took the form of deliberately absurd or extravagant remarks uttered in a tone, and with a mien, of affected seriousness. On one walk he 'gave' to me each tree that we passed, with the reservation that I was not to cut it down or do anything to it, or prevent the previous owners from doing anything to it: with those reservations it was henceforth *mine*. Once when we were walking across Jesus Green at night, he pointed at Cassiopeia and said that it was a 'W' and that it meant *Wittgenstein*. I said that I thought it was an 'M' written upside down and that it meant *Malcolm*. He gravely assured me that I was wrong.

These light-hearted moments were comparatively infrequent. Most commonly his thoughts were sombre. He was constantly depressed, I think, by the impossibility of arriving at understanding in philosophy. But he was worried perhaps even more deeply by the stupidity and heartlessness that present themselves daily in the world in forms that command respect. Of the things that came to his attention in the normal passage of events, hardly any gave him pleasure and many produced in him an emotion that was not far from grief. Often as we walked together he would stop and exclaim 'Oh, my God!', looking at me almost piteously, as if imploring a divine intervention in human events.

One time when we were walking along the river we saw a newsvendor's sign which announced that the German government accused the British government of instigating a recent attempt to assassinate Hitler with a bomb. This was in the autumn of 1939. Wittgenstein said of the German claim: 'It would not surprise me at all if it were true.' I retorted that I could not believe that the top people in the British government would do such a thing. I meant that the British were too civilized and decent to attempt anything so underhand; and I added that such an act was incompatible with the British 'national character'. My remark made Wittgenstein extremely angry. He considered it to be a great stupidity and also an indication that I was not learning anything from the philosophical training that he was trying to give me. He said these things very vehemently, and when I refused to admit that my remark was stupid he would not talk to me any more, and soon after we parted. He had been in the habit of coming to my lodging in Chesterton Road to take me on a short walk with him before his bi-weekly lectures. After this incident he stopped that practice. As will be seen, he kept the episode in mind for several years.

In 1939, G. E. Moore read a paper to the Moral Science Club on an evening when Wittgenstein did not attend. Moore was attempting to prove in his paper that a person can *know* that he has such and such a sensation, e.g. pain. This was in opposition to the view, originating with Wittgenstein, that the concepts of knowledge and certainty have no application to one's own sensations (see *Philosophical Investigations*, § 246). Wittgenstein subsequently heard about Moore's paper and reacted like a war-horse. He came to Moore's at-home, on the following Tuesday. G. H. von Wright, C. Lewy, Smythies and myself were there, and perhaps one or two others. Moore re-read his paper and Wittgenstein immediately attacked it. He was more excited than I ever knew him to be in a discussion. He was full of fire and spoke rapidly and forcefully. He put questions to Moore but frequently did not give Moore a chance to answer. This went on for at least two hours, with Wittgenstein talking almost continuously, Moore getting in a very few remarks, and scarcely a word said by anyone else. Wittgenstein's brilliance and power were impressive and even frightening. When he was discussing this meeting with Smythies some days later, the latter suggested that Wittgenstein had been rude to Moore, in not allowing him to reply. Wittgenstein scoffed at this suggestion as preposterous. But when he next saw Moore he asked, 'Do you think I was rude to you in that discussion?' —to which Moore replied, 'Yes, you were.' I heard that Wittgenstein then made a stiff and reluctant apology.[1]

---

[1] After reading the above, Mr. Yorick Smythies informs me that it is his present recollection that the issue of 'rudeness' was first raised by Moore himself

In the winter of 1939, Moore again read a paper to the Moral Science Club. During the discussion Wittgenstein made a criticism of Moore which I thought had overlooked part of Moore's point, and I expressed this in the discussion by saying that I did not believe that Wittgenstein's criticism had been 'fair' to Moore. Directly after the meeting ended, and while people were still standing about, Wittgenstein walked up to me and said, eyes blazing with anger, 'If you knew anything at all you would know that I am never unfair to anyone. This proves that you have understood absolutely nothing of my lectures.' He turned and walked away. I was thunderstruck.

That night or the next day I talked to Smythies about this incident and explained to him that I had not meant that Wittgenstein was cheating Moore, but merely that he had missed part of Moore's point. Within a day or two I suddenly became ill with 'flu. A young German friend of mine, Tom Rosenmeyer, was worried because there was no one to look after me, and knowing that Wittgenstein and I were close friends, went to tell Wittgenstein about it. He had never met Wittgenstein. When Wittgenstein opened the door of his rooms to Rosenmeyer's knock, the latter simply said, 'Malcolm is ill.' Wittgenstein's immediate reply was, 'Wait. I'll come.' The two came at once. Wittgenstein walked up to my bed and said to me rather severely, 'Smythies thinks that I misunderstood what you meant and if that is so I am sorry.' He then made a fuss of arranging the room more comfortably for me, and undertook to fetch me medicine and food. I felt very happy over this reconciliation. A week or so later I departed for the States. One of the last things that Wittgenstein said before I left was, 'Whatever else you do I hope that you won't marry a lady-philosopher!'

when he accidentally met Wittgenstein in the street, and that Wittgenstein thereafter discussed the matter with either Smythies or Lewy.

A Memoir

So in February 1940 I returned to the United States after one and a half years in Cambridge. Wittgenstein and I kept up a correspondence. I knew that he was fond of detective magazines. They could not be obtained in England during wartime, and periodically I sent some to him from America. He had a preference for a magazine published by Street & Smith, each number of which contained several short detective stories. Wittgenstein acknowledged the arrival of a package of magazines, in a letter from Cambridge.

> Thanks awfully! I'm sure they're grand. My critical eye can see that without having read them, because my critical eye is an X-ray eye & can penetrate from 2 to 4000 pages. That's in fact how I get all my learning.
>
> Now please take it easy! One magazine a month is *ample*. If you send me more I won't have time to do any philosophy. Also please don't waste your money on mags for me, & see that *you* get enough to eat!

In subsequent letters during and after the war he referred to detective magazines more than once:

> It'll be fine to get detective mags from you. There is a terrible scarcity of them now. My mind feels all underfed.
>
> They are *rich* in mental vitamins and calories.
>
> The one way in which the ending of Lend-Lease really hits me is by producing a shortage of detective mags in this country. I can only hope Lord Keynes will make this quite clear in Washington. For I say: if the U.S.A. won't give us detective mags we can't give them philosophy, and so America will be the loser in the end. See?

He compared Street & Smith 'mags' with *Mind*, the international philosophical journal:

> If I read your mags I often wonder how anyone can read

'Mind' with all its impotence & bankruptcy when they could read Street & Smith mags. Well, everyone to his taste.

Two and a half years later he repeated the comparison:

> Your mags are wonderful. How people can read Mind if they could read Street & Smith beats me. If philosophy has anything to do with wisdom there's certainly not a grain of that in Mind, & quite often a grain in the detective stories.

Once Wittgenstein was so pleased with a detective story that he lent it to both Moore and Smythies and wished me to try to find out what else the author had written:

> It may sound crazy, but when I recently re-read the story I liked it again so much that I thought I'd really like to write to the author & thank him. If this is nuts, don't be surprised, for so am I.

Wittgenstein warned me more than once, in his letters, against the temptations to dishonesty that would beset me as a university instructor. When I wrote that I had been awarded the Ph.D. in philosophy, he replied:

> Congratulations to your Ph.D.! And now: may you make good use of it! By that I mean: may you not cheat either yourself or your students. Because, unless I'm very much mistaken, *that's* what will be expected from you. And it will be *very* difficult not to do it, & perhaps impossible; & in this case: may you have the strength *to quit*. This ends today's sermon.

At the end of the letter he said:

> I wish you good, not necessarily clever, thoughts, & decency that won't come out in the wash.

A Memoir

In the fall of 1940 I became an instructor at Princeton, and Wittgenstein wrote:

> I wish you good luck; in particular with your work at the university. The temptation for you to cheat yourself will be *overwhelming* (though I don't mean more for you than for anyone else in your position). *Only by a miracle* will you be able to do decent work in teaching philosophy. Please remember these words, even if you forget everything I've ever said to you; &, if you can help it, don't think that I'm a crank because nobody else will say this to you.

The following summer I told him that Princeton would not re-appoint me for more than one more year and that I might enter the army, to which he answered:

> I am sorry—*honestly*—that you find you won't be able to teach at Princeton after next year. You know what my opinion of teaching philosophy is & I haven't changed it; but I'd like you to quit for the *right* reasons, not for the wrong ones. ('Right' & 'wrong' as I can see it.) I know you'll make a good soldier; still, I hope you won't have to be one. I wish you could live quietly, in a sense, & be in a position to be kind & *understanding* to all sorts of human beings who *need* it! Because we all need this sort of thing very badly.

In the spring of 1942 I resigned my Princeton instructorship and entered the Navy. For three years I wrote to Wittgenstein only infrequently. His replies were always prompt and affectionate. Once he sent me a paper-bound copy of Gottfried Keller's *Hadlaub*, saying:

> I enclose a foul copy of a very wonderful German novel. I couldn't get a decent copy—at least I had no time to look for a better one. German books, as you can imagine, are very difficult to get these days. You may find it rather difficult to

read, &, of course, you mayn't like it; but I hope you will. It's a sort of a Christmas present & I hope you won't mind it being so dirty. The advantage of this is that you can read it down in the engine-room without making it *more* dirty. If you find you like it I'll try to get you the book of which this is only one story. There are five of them called: 'Züricher Novellen', because they're all in some way connected with Zürich: Keller was a Swiss, & one of the greatest German prose writers.

Wittgenstein wrote this letter in November of 1942 from Guy's Hospital in London, where he worked as an orderly for part of the war. During the next year two letters came from the Royal Victoria Infirmary in Newcastle-upon-Tyne, where he was employed in the Clinical Research Laboratory. In one he regrets that

for external & internal reasons I can't do philosophy, for that's the only work that's given me real satisfaction. No other work really bucks me up. I'm extremely busy now & my mind is kept occupied the whole time but at the end of the day I just feel tired & sad.—Well, *perhaps* better times will come again. . . . I very rarely come to Cambridge now, about once every three months. I've given up my rooms in College. I'm supposed, of course, to come back there as a professor after the war, but I must say I can't quite imagine how I'll be able to do it. I wonder if I'll ever be able to teach philosophy again regularly. I rather think I shan't be able.

Three months later he writes from the same place:

I'm still at my old work but may possibly leave here soon as my boss is going into the army & the whole research unit may break up, or get another boss—I am feeling rather lonely here & may try to get to some place where I have someone to talk to. E.g. to Swansea where Rhees is a lecturer in philosophy.

Probably a long time elapsed before I replied to Wittgenstein, because the next letter to me was written nearly a year later in November 1944. He was back at Trinity College, Cambridge. In this letter he revived the incident of our quarrel about the alleged British plot to assassinate Hitler:

Thanks for your letter, dated Nov. 12th, which arrived this morning. I was glad to get it. I thought you had almost forgotten me, or perhaps wished to forget me. I had a particular reason for thinking this. Whenever I thought of you I couldn't help thinking of a particular incident which seemed to me very important. You & I were walking along the river towards the railway bridge & we had a heated discussion in which you made a remark about 'national character' that shocked me by its primitiveness. I then thought: what is the use of studying philosophy if all that it does for you is to enable you to talk with some plausibility about some abstruse questions of logic, etc., & if it does not improve your thinking about the important questions of everyday life, if it does not make you more conscientious than any . . . journalist in the use of the *dangerous* phrases such people use for their own ends. You see, I know that it's difficult to think *well* about 'certainty', 'probability', 'perception', etc. But it is, if possible, still more difficult to think, or *try* to think, really honestly about your life & other peoples lives. And the trouble is that thinking about these things is *not thrilling*, but often downright nasty. And when it's nasty then it's *most* important.—Let me stop preaching. What I wanted to say was this: I'd *very* much like to see you again; but if we meet it would be wrong to avoid talking about serious non-philosophical things. Being timid I don't like clashes, &

particularly not with people I like. But I'd rather have a clash than mere superficial talk.—Well, I thought that when you gradually ceased writing to me it was because you felt that if we were to dig down deep enough we wouldn't be able to see eye to eye in very serious matters. *Perhaps I was quite wrong.* But anyway, if we live to see each other again let's not shirk dipping. You can't think decently if you don't want to hurt yourself. I know all about it because I'm a shirker. . . . Read this letter in a good spirit! Good luck!

Six months later (May 1945) my ship came into Southampton and I obtained leave for thirty-five hours to pay a visit to Cambridge. I saw Wittgenstein in the afternoon and stayed to supper with him. My meeting with him was difficult and painful. He showed no cordiality at all. He did not even greet me. He merely nodded to me, rather grimly, and asked me to sit down (this was in his rooms in Whewell's Court, Trinity). We sat in silence for a long time. When he did begin to talk to me I could not grasp the meaning of his remarks, although I tried with all my might, and I very keenly had the feeling that during my years of naval service my mind had deteriorated. He was cold and severe the whole time. We were not in touch with one another at all. He prepared a supper for us. The *pièce de resistance* was powdered eggs. Wittgenstein asked me whether I cared for them, and, knowing how he valued sincerity, I told him that in truth I thought they were dreadful. He did not like this reply. He muttered something to the effect that if they were good enough for him they were good enough for me. Later he related this incident to Smythies, and (according to Smythies) Wittgenstein took my distaste for powdered eggs as a sign that I had become a snob.

The day after this meeting Wittgenstein received a letter from me which had been written a few weeks before and which was a reply to the letter from which I last quoted above. I think that I may have acknowledged that my remarks about 'national character' were foolish (for I had come to think this), and I must have expressed an appreciation of what he had said in his previous letter to me. In any case he immediately wrote a reply in which he said that had he received the letter 'before I saw you it would have made getting into contact with you rather easier'. He adds:

> I imagine there was a lot on your mind as well as on mine when you were with me. If you write to me, as I hope you will, you might call me by my Christian name & let me do the same. In case this should seem silly, or somehow wrong, to you, just say so frankly. I shan't be hurt.

In a letter written a month later I spoke of the war as a 'boredom', to which he replied:

> I want to say something about the war being a 'boredom'. If a boy said that school was an intense boredom one might answer him that, if he only could get himself to learn what can really be learned there, he would not find it *so* boring. Now forgive me for saying that I can't help believing that an enormous lot can be learnt about human beings in this war— *if* you keep your eyes open. And the better you are at thinking the more you'll get out of what you see. For thinking is *digestion*. If I'm writing in a preaching tone I'm just an ass! but the fact remains that if you're bored a lot it means that your mental digestion isn't what it should be. I think a good remedy for this is sometimes opening your eyes wider. Sometimes a book helps a little, e.g. T's 'Hadshi Murat' wouldn't be bad. If you can't get it in America let me know. I *might* be able to get it here.

In a subsequent letter he said of this book, which he sent to me, 'I hope you'll get a lot out of it, because there is a lot *in* it.'

Of its author, Tolstoy, he remarked, 'There's a *real* man; who has a *right* to write.' In reply to an observation of mine, he says in the same letter, 'Yes, I think I understand why a ship isn't a good place for "thinking"—I mean, *apart* from the fact that you're very busy.'

When Wittgenstein and I later talked about his own service in the First World War he said emphatically that he had never been bored, and I believe that he even said that he did not dislike his army service. He related how he kept a notebook in his rucksack and whenever he had a chance wrote in it the thoughts that compose his first book, the *Tractatus Logico-Philosophicus*.

In the first letter that mentions *Hadji Murat*, there is a reference to the state of preparation of Wittgenstein's new book, the *Philosophical Investigations*:

> My work is going damn slowly. I wish I could get a volume ready for publishing by next autumn; but I probably shan't. I'm a *bloody* bad worker!

Two months later (August 1945), he says:

> I've been working a good deal this last academic year, I mean for myself, & *if* everything goes well I might publish by Christmas. Not that what I've produced is good, but it is now about as good as I can make it. I think when it'll be finished I ought to come into the open with it.

But the next month:

> My work isn't going well; partly because I've contracted some trouble with one of my kidneys. Nothing serious, but it makes me jumpy & bad tempered. (I've always got some excuse.)

A fortnight later:

> My book is gradually nearing its final form, & if you're a

good boy & come to Cambridge I'll let you read it. It'll probably disappoint you. And the truth is: it's pretty lousy. (Not that I could improve on it essentially if I tried for another 100 years.) This, however, doesn't worry me. What I hear about Germany and Austria does. The re-educators of the Germans are doing nicely. Pity there won't be many left to enjoy the fruit of re-education.

He adds:

I'm glad to hear that you're to get out of the Navy before long and I hope you'll come to Cambridge before I make up my mind to resign the absurd job of a prof. of philosophy. It is a kind of living death.

Four months later he says:

My lectures begin in 3 days. I'll talk a lot of rubbish. It would be nice if you could come to Cambridge for an academic year before I resign my job! It might be a good thing, & a good conclusion for my dubious professional career.

I had read Tolstoy's novel *Resurrection* and was greatly impressed by the passage which opens Chapter LIX, beginning with the sentence: 'One of the most widespread superstitions is that every man has his own special definite qualities: that he is kind, cruel, wise, stupid, energetic, apathetic, and so on.' I had quoted the passage to Wittgenstein, which led him to make the following comment:

I once tried to read 'Resurrection' but couldn't. You see, when Tolstoy just tells a story he impresses me infinitely more than when he addresses the reader. When he turns his back to the reader then he seems to me *most* impressive. Perhaps one day we can talk about this. It seems to me his philosophy is most true when it's *latent* in the story.

In another letter he says:

> The other day I read Johnson's 'Life of Pope' & I liked it very much. As soon as I get to Cambridge I'm going to send you a little book 'Prayers & Meditations' by Johnson. You may not like it at all,—on the other hand you may. I do.

He did send it to me, and said in an accompanying note:

> This is the little book I promised to send you. It seems to be out of print so I'm sending you my own copy. I wish to say that normally I can't read any printed prayers but that Johnson's impressed me by being *human*. Perhaps you'll se what I mean if you read them. As likely as not you won't like them *at all*. Because you will probably not look at them from the *angle* from which I see them. (But you might.) If you don't like the book throw it away. Only first cut out the leaf with my dedication. For when I shall become *very* famous it'll become very valuable as an autograph, & your grandchildren may be able to sell it for a lot of 'dough'.

In a letter from Wales he writes:

> My landlord has a modern American translation of the Bible. I dislike the translation of the N.T. (by a man, E. J. Goodspeed) but the translation of the O.T. (by a group of people) makes a lot of things clearer to me & seems to me *well* worth reading. Perhaps you'll see it one day.

I had begun to read Freud, found him fascinating, and said something about this to Wittgenstein. He replied (December 1945):

> I, too, was greatly impressed when I first read Freud. He's extraordinary.—Of course he is full of fishy thinking & his charm & the charm of the subject is so great that you may easily be fooled. He always stresses what great forces in the

mind, what strong prejudices work against the idea of psycho-analysis. But he never says what an enormous charm that idea has for people, just as it has for Freud himself. There may be strong prejudices against uncovering something nasty, but sometimes it is infinitely more *attractive* than it is repulsive. Unless you think *very* clearly psycho-analysis is a dangerous & a foul practice, & it's done no end of harm &, comparatively, very little good. (If you think I'm an old spinster—think again!)—All this, of course, doesn't detract from Freud's extraordinary scientific achievement. Only, extraordinary scientific achievements have a way these days, of being used for the destruction of human beings (I mean their bodies, or their souls, *or their intelligence*). *So hold on to your brains.*

In the spring of 1946, Wittgenstein wrote:

> I feel *very* perturbed in my mind. I haven't done any decent work for ages apart from my classes. They went all right last term. But now my brain feels burnt out, as though only the four walls were left standing, & some charred remains: Let's hope that I'll be in moderately good condition when you'll be here! . . . Tomorrow's my first lecture. *Oh hell!!*

He adds:

> I wish you a better head & a better heart than I have.

Our correspondence terminated because I arrived in Cambridge with my family in the autumn of 1946 to stay for what turned out to be the last year that Wittgenstein held his chair. Wittgenstein came to our house on Searle Street, near Jesus Green, once or twice a week. At first he was suspicious of my wife, whom he had not previously met, as he was of all 'dons' wives', but soon he got over this. When he came to supper he would sometimes insist on washing up the dishes. He had the idea that this could be done more efficiently in the bath tub, where a continuous stream of hot water was available from the geyser. More than once he washed the dishes there, not dissuaded by the severity of the back-bending. Wittgenstein had rigorous standards of cleanliness. He was disturbed if he thought that we were washing up without an adequate supply of soap or clean, hot water. He presented my wife with a dish mop, as an improvement on a dish cloth.

Wittgenstein lectured for three terms that year on topics belonging to the philosophy of psychology. I took notes the first two or three lectures but gave up this practice when I found that Wittgenstein was addressing a great many questions to me and that it was impossible for me to say anything intelligent in reply if I was occupied with writing. (Peter Geach took notes of all the lectures, which are preserved.) Wittgenstein said to me at the conclusion of one of the first classes that he expected me to take an active part in the discussions. I resolved to do my best, and throughout the year I made a great effort to follow his thoughts during those meetings, an exertion that left my mind utterly exhausted at the end of two hours. The classes were even more exciting for me than they had been seven years before. I understood Wittgenstein's ideas better, although still not well, and the astonishing depth and originality of his thinking was strikingly evident to me. Frequently after the lectures I wrote down brief résumés of what I had understood. I will transcribe from my notes of a few lectures in order to give samples of the sort of questions that Wittgenstein asked and the thoughts that he produced in reply to them. These notes were not intended to be verbatim, although sometimes they may have been partly so. They were merely summaries of my recollections of the ideas that impressed me most in each lecture. These summaries were not set down until several hours after the lecture and frequently not until a day or two later.

A Memoir

In one lecture he talked about the notion of an *explanation* of the uses of an expression:

> In supposing that the colour red (and also the pheno-
> menon of thinking something to oneself) is something
> specific and indescribable, one supposes that one could learn
> what red is simply by seeing a red image. But what if I hit
> you on the head, and thereafter you were able to use the
> word 'red' correctly? Would this be an explanation of what
> red is? Of course not. An explanation is not *anything* that
> produces understanding. A key is not *anything* which opens
> a door.
>
> A man might say: 'I know this book is red, because I have
> a mental impression of red.' But how does he know that he
> remembers the impression correctly? And how does he *com-
> pare* the impression with the book?
>
> An explanation cannot be something private. It must be
> public. An explanation must provide a technique for getting
> somewhere. It must show the way. It must provide a method
> for using the word.
>
> So if someone says 'I can show myself what thinking is,
> although I can't show anyone else,' we reply that he may do
> something which makes it possible for him to use the word
> correctly, but that this may not be at all what we call
> 'explaining' or 'showing'.
>
> It may be objected to our method as follows: 'If someone
> asks what *time* is, you ask in return, "How do we measure
> time?" But time and the measurement of time are two dif-
> ferent things. It is as if someone asked "What is a book?" and
> you replied, "How does one obtain a book?" '
>
> This objection conceives that we know what *time* is, and
> we know what *measuring* is, *so* we know what measuring
> time is. But this is not true. If I have taught you to measure

lengths, and then say, 'Now go ahead and measure time,' this will mean nothing.

Consider a tribe of people who measure lengths of fields by striding along and counting their steps. If different results are obtained for the same field, they think nothing of it!—even if payments depend on the results of the counting! If you come along and say that you have a better method which uses a tape measure, they might be quite uninterested. They might say: 'What a queer method that uses troublesome gadgets and always gets the same result! Our method is much better.'

The notion of a more accurate measurement does not enter into their lives, and so the notion of the *real* length does not either. If we say 'They *must* have the notion of a *real* length,' this is only because we imagine a more complicated life in which one method of measuring is preferred to another. But that is not their life.

Another time Wittgenstein discussed our knowledge of our bodily posture and the position of our limbs:

In order to move my arm voluntarily I must know what position it is in and whether I have moved it. Now how do I know what the position of my hand is, when I am not looking at it or feeling it with the other hand? How do I know, e.g., that my fingers are bent? There is a temptation to say 'I feel that they are bent.' This is a peculiar reply. For do you always have a certain feeling when your fingers are bent in that way; have you always noticed that feeling; and what feeling is it?

The feeling that my fingers are bent: is it subject to more and less, to *degrees*, as are feelings of temperature and pressure? No. This may show that 'I feel that my fingers are bent' means nothing different from 'I know that they are bent.' If we try to say what feelings of temperature, pressure, etc. make up this feeling that my fingers are bent, we sha that it is not easy to say what they are, and furthermore we see that we rarely have them.

There *could* be cases in which I knew the position of my hand by a certain feeling. Also it may be true that if my hand were anaesthetized I should *not* know its position. But from this it does not follow that normally I know the position of my hand by certain sensations.

The question, 'How do I know my fingers are bent?' is just like the question, 'How do I know where my pain is?' I don't need to be shown where my pain is. My pointing gesture and verbal description *locates* the pain. Likewise I don't need to find out the posture of my body.

The notes from another meeting read as follows:

There is a philosophical question as to what one *really* *sees*. Does one really see depth, or physical objects, or sadness, or a face, etc.? There is a temptation to say that all of this is 'interpretation', 'hypothesis', etc., and that what one *really* sees is a flat surface of coloured patches.

But if I am required to describe what I see, I do it with physical-object expressions: e.g. 'I see the top of a tan table; on it is an ink bottle towards the right end,' etc. I would not be able to describe it by referring only to coloured patches.

It might be thought that although I cannot describe it in words, at least I could paint it. But the fact is that I can hardly paint at all unless I know what physical *objects* I am painting.

A criterion of whether a painting is a correct representation of what I saw is that I *say* it is. But some things might be changed in the painting and yet I should still say that it is exactly what I saw.

Ludwig Wittgenstein

We have the idea of an *ideal* model or an *ideal* description of what one sees at any time. But no such ideal description exists. There are numerous sorts of things which we call 'descriptions' of what we see. They are all *rough*. And 'rough' here does *not* mean 'approximation'. We have the mistaken idea that there is a certain exact description of what one sees at any given moment.

In one lecture he made some general remarks about his philosophical procedure:

What I give is the morphology of the use of an expression. I show that it has kinds of uses of which you had not dreamed. In philosophy one feels *forced* to look at a concept in a certain way. What I do is to suggest, or even invent, other ways of looking at it. I suggest possibilities of which you had not previously thought. You thought that there was one possibility, or only two at most. But I made you think of others. Furthermore, I made you see that it was absurd to expect the concept to conform to those narrow possibilities. Thus your mental cramp is relieved, and you are free to look around the field of use of the expression and to describe the different kinds of uses of it.

In addition to attending Wittgenstein's lectures, I met with him privately one afternoon a week. Wittgenstein proposed that we should read his book together. He lent me a typescript copy of it. It was the writing that was posthumously published as Part I of the *Investigations*. Our procedure at the weekly meeting was the following: We sat in his living-room with our canvas chairs close together so that both of us could read the typescript. Starting at the beginning of the work, Wittgenstein first read a sentence aloud in German, then translated it into English, then made some remarks to me about the meaning of it. He then went to the next sentence; and so on. At the following meeting he started at the place where we had last stopped. At first I was flattered by this treatment. Wittgenstein once said to me, 'The reason I am doing this is so there will be at least one person who will understand my book when it is published.' After a time, however, I began to feel that this method was too confining. I wished to have discussions that would start from various philosophical questions that were currently puzzling to me. And, indeed, he gradually relaxed this procedure, and our discussions became more free.

Once when we were together he made a striking observation about philosophy: 'A person caught in a philosophical confusion is like a man in a room who wants to get out but doesn't know how. He tries the window but it is too high. He tries the chimney but it is too narrow. And if he would only *turn around*, he would see that the door has been open all the time!' This comment is related to remarks in the *Investigations*, § 108, § 123, § 309. (Wittgenstein once observed in a lecture that there is a similarity between his conception of philosophy (e.g. 'the problems are solved, not by giving new information, but by arranging what we have always known', *Investigations*, § 109; 'the work of the philosopher consists in assembling reminders for a particular purpose', ibid., § 127) and the Socratic doctrine that knowledge is reminiscence: although he believed that there were also other things involved in the latter.)

After about two hours of reading or discussion, we would go for a walk and then have tea at Lyons, or in the restaurant above the Regal cinema. Sometimes he came to my house in Searle Street for supper. Once after supper, Wittgenstein, my wife and I went for a walk on Midsummer Common. We talked about the movements of the bodies of the solar system. It occurred to Wittgenstein that the three of us should represent the movements of the sun, earth, and moon, relative to one another. My wife was the sun and maintained a steady pace across the meadow; I was the earth and circled her at a trot. Wittgenstein took the most strenuous part of all, the moon, and ran around me while I circled my wife. Wittgenstein entered into this game with great enthusiasm and seriousness, shouting instructions at us as he ran. He became quite breathless and dizzy with exhaustion.

Wittgenstein was fond of the fairs that came occasionally to Midsummer Common. He liked to roll pennies for prizes. He refused to try to direct the course of the penny, even closing his eyes before releasing it, because 'everything must be left to chance'. He was somewhat disapproving when my wife tried to direct the motion of her penny. He persuaded me to throw balls at targets, was excited while I did so, and afterwards extolled my modest prowess in extravaga..t terms.

Once when we were conversing Wittgenstein was delighted to learn that I knew Tolstoy's *Twenty-Three Tales*. He had an extremely high opinion of these stories. He questioned me closely to find out whether I had understood the moral of the one entitled *How Much Land Does A Man Need?* Wittgenstein had been stiff with me at the beginning of the conversation because he was displeased with me for a reason I have forgotten. But when he discovered that I had read, understood and valued Tolstoy's stories, he became friendly and animated. Wittgenstein also admired the writings of Dostoievsky. He had read *The Brothers Karamazov* an extraordinary number of times; but he once said that *The House of the Dead* was Dostoievsky's greatest work.

Wittgenstein was persuaded to have weekly 'at-homes' during term-time that year. They were on Saturday afternoons from five to seven. Philosophical discussions occurred on questions raised by those attending. Although these meetings were less formal than his classes, in the sense that coming late was not an offence and consistent attendance was not required, nevertheless their atmosphere was serious to the point of solemnity. Normally about half-a-dozen people came. As we arrived one by one we found Wittgenstein sitting in silence in his canvas deck-chair, greeting no one, his face stern, apparently engrossed in serious reflection. No one dared to break the silence with an idle remark. We sat quietly as if absorbed in thought. Peter Geach once observed that it had the appearance of a Quaker prayer meeting. It took nerve to shatter this silence by introducing a topic. As soon as someone did, however, Wittgenstein was all attention—trying to grasp the meaning of the question, expanding or reformulating it, connecting it with other questions that at first seemed unrelated, and always, by his passionate intensity and force, endowing the question with dramatic interest. Topics in aesthetics were perhaps the most frequent at these at-homes, and the depth and richness of Wittgenstein's thinking about art were very exciting.

At one of the at-homes, Wittgenstein related a riddle for the purpose of throwing some light on the nature of philosophy. It went as follows: Suppose that a cord was stretched tightly around the earth at the equator. Now suppose that a piece one yard long was added to the cord. If the cord was kept taut and circular in form, how much above the surface of the earth would it be? Without stopping to work it out, everyone present was inclined to say that the distance of the cord from the surface of the earth would be so *minute* that it would be imperceptible. But this is wrong. The actual distance would be nearly six inches. Wittgenstein declared that this is the *kind* of mistake that occurs in philosophy. It consists in being *misled by a picture*. In the riddle the picture that misleads us is the comparison of the length of the additional piece with the length of the whole cord. The picture itself is correct enough: for a piece one yard long would be an insignificant fraction of the length of the whole cord. But we are misled by it to draw a wrong conclusion. A similar thing happens in philosophy: we are constantly deceived by mental pictures which are in themselves correct. Another striking illustration of a misleading picture that Wittgenstein gave, was a drawing of the earth as a ball with the people at the antipodes upside down and ourselves rightside up. The drawing, he said, does not misrepresent; yet it tempts us to think that the inhabitants of the antipodes are *beneath* us, and that they really hang head downwards. (This illustration is discussed in the *Investigations*, § 351.)

Wittgenstein devoted a great deal of time to students that year. There were his two weekly classes of two hours each, his weekly at-home of two hours, a whole afternoon spent with me, another whole afternoon spent with Elizabeth Anscombe and W. A. Hijab, and finally the weekly evening meeting of the Moral Science Club which he usually attended. The atmosphere of the discussions at the latter was extremely disagreeable to Wittgenstein. He went only out of a sense of duty, thinking that he ought to do what he could to help make the discussions as decent as possible. After the paper was read, Wittgenstein was invariably the first one to speak, and he completely dominated the discussion as long as he was present. He believed, as he told me, that it was not good for the Club that he should always play such a prominent role there, but on the other hand it was quite impossible for him not to participate in the discussions with his characteristic force. His solution was to leave the meetings at the end of an hour and a half or two hours. The result was that the discussion was exciting and important while Wittgenstein was present, but trivial, flat, and anti-climactic after he left.

In all of these meetings: lectures, at-homes, private discussions and Club meetings, Wittgenstein gave his thoughts without stint. There was never any attempt by him to preserve his researches in secrecy. Furthermore, in every one of these discussions he was trying to *create*. The force of will and spirit that he exerted was awesome. As he struggled to work through a problem one frequently felt that one was in the presence of real suffering. Wittgenstein liked to draw an analogy between philosophical thinking and swimming: just as one's body has a natural tendency towards the surface and one has to make an *exertion* to get to the *bottom*—so it is with thinking. In talking about human greatness, he once remarked that he thought that the measure of a man's greatness would be in terms of what his work *cost* him. There is no doubt that Wittgenstein's philosophical labours cost him a great deal.

Wittgenstein had an extraordinary gift for divining the thoughts of the person with whom he was engaged in discussion. While the other struggled to put his thought into words Wittgenstein would perceive what it was and state it for him. This power of his, which sometimes seemed uncanny, was made possible, I am sure, by his own prolonged and continuous researches. He knew what someone else was thinking because he had *himself* travelled innumerable times through those twists and turns of reasoning. He once remarked to me that it was very unlikely that anyone in his classes should think of something of which he had not already thought. This was not braggadocio.

His heavy programme of that year put him under a great strain. He was sometimes troubled as to whether he should meet still other demands. For example, one man had come half-way around the world, at considerable sacrifice, in order to study with Wittgenstein. He wished to have private discussions with Wittgenstein, in addition to the lectures. Wittgenstein worried over this request. He felt under some obligation to meet it: on the other hand, he believed that he must conserve his strength. I think that he finally turned down the

Ludwig Wittgenstein

request. But it was typical of him to consider such a matter always in the light of what his *duty* was.

On the outskirts of Cambridge was a camp where German prisoners-of-war were confined. Wittgenstein had been a prisoner in the First War and was anxious to do something that might help to make the lives of these men more tolerable. He took me with him on a visit to the camp. He received permission to confer with a prisoners' representative. As a result of this conference I believe that Wittgenstein subsequently provided some musical instruments and music for the prisoners.

An incident occurred that winter which greatly excited and upset Wittgenstein. A certain philosopher published in a literary and critical journal an article that purported to give a popular account of contemporary British philosophy. Of Wittgenstein the article said that the nature of his philosophical work since the publication of *Tractatus* was unknown; but that if one were to judge from the writings of a leading disciple, philosophy, in Wittgenstein's hands, had become a kind of psycho-analysis. Someone showed this article to Wittgenstein and he was extremely angered by it. He said that the author merely pretended to be ignorant of his work. What made Wittgenstein furious was not only his belief in the author's dishonesty, but also the implication that Wittgenstein kept the nature of his work a secret. He said that he had always regarded his lectures as a form of publication. (I should mention here that two volumes of material which he had dictated to students, known as 'The Blue Book' and 'The Brown Book', had been circulating privately, in mimeograph or typescript form, for more than ten years and had been widely read by British philosophers.) I believe another thing that angered him was the suggestion that in his conception philosophy was a form of psycho-analysis, a suggestion that I had heard him explicitly attack, on two occasions, as based on a confusion. 'They are different techniques,' he had said.

This article threw Wittgenstein into a great state for several days. He asked me whether I would publish a reply to it. My answer was that I did not have the least idea what form a reply could take. Wittgenstein disliked this answer. He wanted to know whether I would undertake to defend Moore, in print, if someone were to say false and unjust things about *his* philosophical work. I felt compelled to say that I would. Wittgenstein then exclaimed that this confirmed what he had always suspected—namely, that his friends regarded *him* as 'Vogelfrei': that is, as an outlaw, a bird at whom anyone had a right to shoot. I believe that Wittgenstein asked both Anscombe and Smythies whether they would publish a reply to the article, but did not get an affirmative answer. To the former he repeated the expression 'Vogelfrei'. For two or three days Wittgenstein was in a real frenzy about the matter. He even contemplated sending a reply of his own to the same journal. Also he talked seriously of taking his typescript (Part I of the *Investigations*) to the Cambridge University Press for immediate publication. After a few days he calmed down. He said that he was not going to be 'stampeded' into publishing prematurely. He did write a private note to the author of the article, in which he said that he believed that the latter had more knowledge of the nature of Wittgenstein's philosophical researches than he had represented in the article. Wittgenstein received a polite and deferential note in reply, and the incident was closed.

Wittgenstein expressed more than once the fear that his writings would be destroyed by fire. He related with horror how the great historian, Mommsen, had lost a manuscript volume of his History of Rome in that way. Wittgenstein purchased a light steel safe in which he kept his notebooks and manuscripts in his living-room at Trinity. He said more than once that though he doubted that he would publish any of this work in his lifetime he definitely wished to have his book (Part I of the *Investigations*) published after his death. On the other hand, he once exclaimed to me with vehemence that he would gladly see all of his writings destroyed if along with them would vanish the publications of his pupils and disciples. He was sometimes visited by the fear that when his work was finally published posthumously the learned world might believe that he had obtained his ideas from philosophers whom he had taught, because there might be some resemblances between his work and those writings of theirs that had been published before his own. He asked me very earnestly if I would defend him, after his death, from any such claim or rumour that might arise, and I told him that I would. His anxiety on this matter is reflected in the preface of the *Investigations*: 'For more than *one* reason what I publish here will have points of contact with what other people are writing today—If my remarks do not bear a stamp which marks them as mine—I do not wish to lay any further claim to them as my property.'

Wittgenstein had strong feelings about plagiarism. He gave me an account of his relationship with a certain man, about which there had been many rumours. Wittgenstein said that Moritz Schlick, this man, and himself had met together for some philosophical discussions, and that he had set forth some of his ideas while they took notes. Sometime later he had seen a paper of this man's which had been accepted for publication and which was not only based on Wittgenstein's ideas but even used Wittgenstein's own illustrations. This article did contain an acknowledgement but phrased in such a manner as to suggest that while the author had derived a certain amount of stimulation from talks with Wittgenstein the main work was, of course, his own. Wittgenstein was extremely incensed. He said that he took the matter up with Schlick, who was 'a decent human being', and that the latter promised to do something about it. But there occurred just then the sudden death of Schlick by assassination, and so the paper was published without adequate acknowledgement of indebtedness.

Wittgenstein was almost as much angered by imperfect representations of his thoughts as by the plagiarism of them. He told me of an incident involving a young lady, who had attended his lectures. She wrote an article which was intended to present Wittgenstein's views on a certain topic. She submitted it to Moore, the editor of *Mind*, and also showed it to Wittgenstein. Wittgenstein thought it was very bad and told her that she *could not* publish it. When she persisted in her intention to publish, Wittgenstein went to Moore to persuade him not to print it. He said to Moore: 'You attended those lectures. You know that her account of them is bad!' According to Wittgenstein, Moore admitted that 'It wasn't good,' but was not dissuaded from publishing the piece. It was clear to me that Wittgenstein had been very much vexed and excited by this incident. Probably it is one of the things to which he refers in the preface of the *Investigations*: '. . . I was obliged to learn that my results (which I had communicated in lectures, typescripts and discussions), variously misunderstood, more or less mangled or watered down, were in circulation. This stung my vanity and I had difficulty in quieting it.'

Although considerations of reputation were certainly not unknown to his nature, and could even become violent, as in the episodes just related, it must be remembered, on the other hand, that Wittgenstein purposely lived in obscurity, discouraging all attempts to make him into a celebrity or public figure, which otherwise he would certainly have become.

His conception of the value of his own work would not be easy to describe. In the preface of the *Investigations* he says that it is not 'a good book', and this remark was not an affectation of modesty. He certainly believed that the work might have been made better, although not by himself. To Dr. Louise Mooney, who treated him when he was ill in the summer of 1949, and to whom he talked a little bit about his work, he exclaimed: 'Maybe it is all mistaken; maybe it is all wrong.' But this was not a characteristic attitude. He expounded and defended his ideas in argument with confidence and power. He did not think of the central conceptions of his philosophy as *possibly* in error. He certainly believed, most of the time, that he had produced an important advance in philosophy. Yet I think that he was inclined to feel that the importance of this advance might be exaggerated by those who were too close to it. This feeling is probably reflected in his choice of Nestroy's remark for the motto of the *Investigations*: 'Überhaupt hat der Fortschritt das an sich, dass er viel grösser ausschaut, als er wirklich ist.' (It is in the nature of every advance, that it appears much greater than it actually is.)

With regard to the question of what the future would hold for his work—whether it would disappear without leaving a mark, or whether, if it continued to live, it would prove any help to mankind—he was in doubt. Freud once remarked in a letter: 'As to the question of the value of my work and its influence on the future development of science I myself find it very hard to form an opinion. Sometimes I believe in it; sometimes I doubt. I don't think there is any way of predicting it; perhaps God himself doesn't yet know' (Ernest Jones, *Sigmund Freud,* London, 1955, Vol. II, p. 446). I think that these sentences would also serve very well to express Wittgenstein's attitude towards his own work, with the exception that his inclination to pessimism was stronger than Freud's. I do not believe that Wittgenstein ever thought of his work as *great*.

Wittgenstein sometimes doubted his friends, as illustrated by the 'Vogelfrei' incident. He suspected that they were not

attached to him by affection but rather by their interest in him
as a source of philosophical inspiration. He once told me that
he had given away his fortune, when a young man, so that he
would not have any friends on account of it, but now he
feared that he had friends for the sake of the philosophy they
could get out of him. He wanted friends who were not trying
to *get anything* out of him. Another time he said: 'Although I
cannot *give* affection, I have a great *need* for it.' Human kindness, human concern, was for him a far more important
attribute in a person than intellectual power or cultivated taste.
He related with pleasure an incident that happened to him in
Wales. He had taken lodgings in the home of a preacher. The
first time that Wittgenstein presented himself at this house the
lady of the house had inquired of Wittgenstein whether he would
like some tea, and whether he would also like this and that other
thing. Her husband called to her from another room: 'Do not
ask; *give*!' Wittgenstein was most favourably impressed by this
exclamation. A characteristic remark that Wittgenstein would
make when referring to someone who was notably generous or
kind or honest was 'He is a *human being*!'—thus implying that
most people fail even to be human.

Undoubtedly Wittgenstein did greatly need human warmth
and affection and he was enormously appreciative of any simple
kindness. But a friendly relationship with him was very exacting. He could rebuke a friend with extreme harshness. He had
a tendency to be suspicious of motives and character. Sometimes his judgements were precipitous and in error. But on the
whole he formed acute and realistic estimates of his friends. As
Smythies remarked, when Wittgenstein gave one a lashing one
usually had it coming. One learned things about oneself from
Wittgenstein's rebukes. He was particularly hard on all forms
of vanity, affectation, or complacency.

But Wittgenstein could be excessively severe with a friend

as some of the previous incidents may have shown. Another illustration, perhaps amusing, is the following: In his rooms at Trinity he kept a small, potted flowering plant. When he left Cambridge between terms to go to Wales, he left this plant at our house. I am afraid that we were negligent, sometimes leaving the plant too near an electric heater. It began to look sickly and the leaves and buds gradually dropped off. When Wittgenstein came back to Cambridge I returned the plant to his rooms, although it was then quite dead. A few days later he and my wife had a chance meeting on the street, the first since his departure for Wales six weeks previously. Without any greeting he said severely: 'I see that you know nothing about plants!' and walked off without another word. My wife was upset. When he next came to our house no further mention of the plant was made.

It was always a strain to be with Wittgenstein. Not only were the intellectual demands of his conversation very great, but there was also his severity, his ruthless judgements, his tendency to be censorious, and his depression. Each time that I spent several hours with him in the winter of 1946-7 my mind would be exhausted and my nerves frayed. My typical feeling was that I could not bear to see him again for some days.

Several times that winter Wittgenstein expressed a doubt that he would continue to serve in his chair. Undoubtedly the idea of being a *professional* philosopher was very repugnant to him. Universities and academic life he disliked intensely. He was exhausted by his strenuous programme of lectures and discussions. Perhaps more importantly, he believed that his influence as a teacher was largely harmful. He was disgusted and pained by what he observed of the half-understanding of his philosophical ideas, and of a tendency towards a shallow cleverness in his students. He felt himself to be a failure as a teacher. This, I believe, was a source of constant torment to him. In his lectures he would sometimes exclaim in a tone of real suffering: 'I am a dreadful teacher!' He once concluded a year's lectures with this sentence: 'The only seed that I am likely to sow is a certain jargon.'

Apart from other things, I think that there was indeed something in the content of his philosophy that, improperly assimilated, had and still has an unfortunate effect on those influenced by it. I refer to his conception that words are not used with 'fixed' meanings (*Investigations,* § 79), that concepts do not have 'sharp boundaries' (ibid., § 68, § 76). This teaching, I believe, produced a tendency in his students to assume that precision and thoroughness were not required in their own thinking. From this tendency nothing but slovenly philosophical work could result.

The considerations in favour of resigning his chair were acquiring more and more force in Wittgenstein's mind. This was particularly revealed by an incident involving a certain philosopher, with whom I was acquainted. The latter wrote me in the winter of 1946-7 that he wished to spend the next year in Cambridge and wondered whether he could obtain permission to attend Wittgenstein's lectures. I took the matter up with Wittgenstein. As I recall, he wrote directly to this man, giving him permission. But Wittgenstein asked me to write to him too and caution him that it was not impossible that he would resign his chair before the next academic year. Wittgenstein wished me, rather than himself, to convey this warning, in order not to give rise to rumour. I did as he wished. Then in the summer of 1947 he did go to see the Vice-Chancellor in order to submit his resignation. But there he was informed that he was entitled to a term of sabbatical leave; and he was persuaded to take leave during the Michaelmas term of 1947 and to postpone the question of his resignation. He then asked me to inform the above man of the change in his plans, and to say that so far as was then known Wittgenstein would lecture during the Lent term, although the possibility that he would resign still existed. I did as requested. When in the autumn Wittgenstein did resign his chair, the man in question was greatly incensed and made (as will be seen) absurd and unjust accusations against Wittgenstein, as if under the impression that the latter had deliberately misled him, or as if Wittgenstein was under an obligation to remain in his chair because this man had expected to attend his lectures. The fact is that Wittgenstein had shown unusual consideration.

Wittgenstein was widely regarded by people who did not know him, as a mysterious and eccentric figure. He was the object not only of hostility but also of innumerable fantastic rumours. Once in Cambridge I heard one undergraduate in earnestness inform another that Wittgenstein delivered his lectures while lying on the floor and gazing at the ceiling. When he was living in my house in the States it was reported that his residence was a barn and that I was the only person who could have access to him. And later when he was living in a cottage on the Irish coast I heard a grave rumour that he was herding goats in Turkey.

An undergraduate who lived a floor or two below Wittgenstein's rooms in Whewell's Court, kept a piano on which he frequently practised. The sounds penetrated to Wittgenstein's rooms and almost drove him mad, especially when the music was familiar to him. It was impossible for him to think when he heard the piano. He solved this problem in a characteristic way. He obtained a large, second-hand electric fan which produced a uniform noise in sufficient volume to drown the piano. I was in his rooms for discussions several times when the fan was going, but found the roar of it completely distracting, whereas Wittgenstein was not bothered in the least.

The mathematical physicist, Freeman Dyson, then an undergraduate, lived in the set of rooms adjacent to Wittgenstein's. Once Wittgenstein invited him to tea. The conversation, as Dyson told me, was first about the nature of Dyson's studies. Then the latter, out of politeness, asked Wittgenstein what the nature of his own work was. Wittgenstein was at first wary, wanting to know whether Dyson was a 'journalist'. Assured that he was not, Wittgenstein then did talk to Dyson about the nature of philosophy and his own part in it. Dyson recalled one anecdote of Wittgenstein's which is of considerable interest: One day when Wittgenstein was passing a field where a football game was in progress the thought first struck him that in language we play *games* with *words*. A central idea of his philosophy, the notion of a 'language-game', apparently had its genesis in this incident. Dyson also recalled his last encounter with Wittgenstein. It was the end of the May term of 1946–7 and Dyson was packing his trunk at the bottom of the stairs in Whewell's Court. Wittgenstein, whom he had not seen for several weeks, came down the stairs with his walking stick, raincoat and tweed cap. He nodded to Dyson and started to walk past, but then stopped and said: 'My mind is getting stupider and stupider!' He then walked off without another word.

What the relationship of Wittgenstein was to the famous 'verification principle' ('The meaning of a statement is its method of verification') of Logical Positivism has often been a subject of curiosity. Wittgenstein told me an anecdote that sheds some light on this. The philosopher and psychologist, G. F. Stout, came to Cambridge for a brief visit and Wittgenstein invited him to tea. (My impression is that this was in the early 30's.) Stout said to Wittgenstein that he had heard that Wittgenstein had something interesting and important to say about *verification*, and that he would like very much to know about it. Both of them knew that Stout had to leave very shortly to catch a train and Wittgenstein would not ordinarily, as he told me, have tried to make any kind of philosophical remark in such circumstances. But Stout's seriousness and genuine desire to understand Wittgenstein's teaching on this point so impressed him that he related to Stout the following parable: Imagine that there is a town in which the policemen are required to obtain information from each inhabitant, e.g. his age, where he came from, and what work he does. A record is kept of this information and some use is made of it. Occasionally when a policeman questions an inhabitant he discovers that the latter does not do *any* work. The policeman enters this fact on the record, because *this too* is a useful piece of information about the man!

The application of the parable is, I think, that if you do not understand a statement, then to discover that it has no verification is an important piece of information about it and makes you understand it better. That is to say, you understand it *better*; you do not find out that there is nothing to understand.

During his final year as a professor Wittgenstein used to visit Moore about once every fortnight. Wittgenstein respected Moore's honesty and seriousness, and once he said that Moore was 'deep'. At the same time talks with Moore almost always depressed him, because Moore was so 'child-like'. Wittgenstein once remarked that what Moore primarily did, as a philosopher, was to 'destroy premature solutions' of philosophical problems, which struck me as an acute characterization. But he added that he did not believe that Moore would *recognize* a *correct* solution if he were presented with one. He said that he had attended Moore's lectures only a few times, when he was a student at Cambridge before World War I, because he could not bear the repetitiousness that always characterized them. He once remarked that the only work of Moore's that greatly impressed him was his discovery of the peculiar kind of nonsense involved in such a sentence as, e.g. 'It is raining but I don't believe it.' (This is referred to as 'Moore's paradox' in Sec. x, Part II, of the *Investigations*.) But he admitted that Moore's 'defence of common sense' was an important idea. He observed that if one were trying to find exactly the right words to express a fine distinction of thought, Moore was absolutely the best person to consult.

Wittgenstein related to me an anecdote about Moore that, he thought, exhibited what was most admirable in Moore's character: Moore had been working hard on his lecture entitled 'Proof of an External World', which he was to deliver before the British Academy in London. He was very dissatisfied with the concluding part of it, but he had not been able to revise it in a way that satisfied him. On the day of the lecture, as he got ready to leave his house in Cambridge to catch the London train, Mrs. Moore said to him, 'Don't worry; I'm sure they'll like it.' To which Moore replied: 'If they *do* they'll be *wrong*!' I believe that this incident reveals that in Moore which Wittgenstein regarded as 'deep'.

Moore's health was quite good in 1946–7, but before that he had suffered a stroke and his doctor had advised that he should not become greatly excited or fatigued. Mrs. Moore enforced this prescription by not allowing Moore to have a philosophical discussion with anyone for longer than one hour and a half. Wittgenstein was extremely vexed by this regulation. He believed that Moore should not be supervised by his wife. He should discuss as long as he liked. If he became very excited or tired and had a stroke and died—well, that would be a decent way to die: with his boots on. Wittgenstein felt that it was unseemly that Moore, with his great love for truth, should be forced to break off a discussion before it had reached its proper end. I think that Wittgenstein's reaction to this regulation was very characteristic of his outlook on life. A human being should do the thing for which he has a talent with all of his energy his life long, and should never relax this devotion to his job merely in order to prolong his existence. This platonistic attitude was manifested again two years later when Wittgenstein, feeling that he was losing his own talent, questioned whether he should continue to live.

Wittgenstein more than once expressed admiration of the keenness of Bertrand Russell's intellect when the two of them worked together on problems of logic before the First World War. Russell was extremely 'bright', is how he put it: Moore, in comparison, was less so. Wittgenstein recalled with pleasure that one day, when Russell and himself had finished several hours of hard work together, Russell had exclaimed, 'Logic is hell!' This exclamation characterized Wittgenstein's attitude towards his own philosophical labours. Wittgenstein believed that the Theory of Descriptions was Russell's most important production, and he once remarked that it must have been an enormously difficult undertaking for him. But in 1946 Wittgenstein had a poor opinion of Russell's contemporary philosophical writings. 'Russell isn't going to kill himself doing philosophy now,' he said with a smile. I noticed that on the infrequent occasions when both Russell and Wittgenstein were at the Moral Science Club, Wittgenstein was deferential to Russell in the discussion as I never knew him to be with anyone else.

Wittgenstein related to me two anecdotes pertaining to the *Tractatus*, which perhaps I should record, although he also told them to several other persons. One has to do with the origination of the central idea of the *Tractatus*—that a proposition is a *picture*. This idea came to Wittgenstein when he was serving in the Austrian army in the First War. He saw a newspaper that described the occurrence and location of an automobile accident by means of a diagram or map. It occurred to Wittgenstein that this map was a proposition and that therein was revealed the essential nature of propositions—namely, to *picture* reality.

The other incident has to do with something that precipitated the destruction of this conception. Wittgenstein and P. Sraffa, a lecturer in economics at Cambridge, argued together a great deal over the ideas of the *Tractatus*. One day (they were riding, I think, on a train) when Wittgenstein was insisting that a proposition and that which it describes must have the same 'logical form', the same 'logical multiplicity', Sraffa made a gesture, familiar to Neapolitans as meaning something like disgust or contempt, of brushing the underneath of his chin with an outward sweep of the finger-tips of one hand. And he asked: 'What is the logical form of *that*?' Sraffa's example produced in Wittgenstein the feeling that there was an absurdity in the insistence that a proposition and what it describes must have the same 'form'. This broke the hold on him of the conception that a proposition must literally be a 'picture' of the reality it describes.[1]

Wittgenstein frequently said to me disparaging things about the *Tractatus*. I am sure, however, that he still regarded it as an important work. For one thing, he was greatly concerned in the *Investigations* to refute the errors of the former book. Also he told me once that he really thought that in the *Tractatus* he had provided a perfected account of a view that is the *only* alternative to the viewpoint of his later work. For another thing, he definitely wanted the *Tractatus* to be republished jointly with his newer writings. As he says in the preface of the *Investigations*, it

[1] Professor G. H. von Wright informs me that Wittgenstein related this incident to him somewhat differently: the question at issue, according to Wittgenstein, was whether every proposition must have a 'grammar', and Sraffa asked Wittgenstein what the 'grammar' of that gesture was. In describing the incident to von Wright, Wittgenstein did not mention the phrases 'logical form' or 'logical multiplicity'.

'seemed to me that I should publish those old thoughts and the new ones together: that the latter could be seen in the right light only by contrast with and against the background of my old ways of thinking.'

At this point I should like to say what I can on the difficult subject of Wittgenstein's attitude towards religion. He told me that in his youth he had been contemptuous of it, but that at about the age of twenty-one something had caused a change in him. In Vienna he saw a play that was mediocre drama, but in it one of the characters expressed the thought that no matter what happened in the world, nothing bad could happen to *him*—he was independent of fate and circumstances. Wittgenstein was struck by this stoic thought; for the first time he saw the possibility of religion. He said that during his service in the First War he came across Tolstoy's writings on the Gospels, which made a great impression on him.

Wittgenstein says in the *Tractatus*: 'Not *how* the world is, is the mystical, but *that* it is' (§ 6.44). I believe that a certain feeling of amazement that *anything should exist at all,* was sometimes experienced by Wittgenstein, not only during the *Tractatus* period, but also when I knew him.[1] Whether this feeling has anything to do with religion is not clear to me. But Wittgenstein did once say that he thought that he could understand the conception of God, in so far as it is involved in one's

---

[1] After writing this sentence I learned that Wittgenstein once read a paper on Ethics (at a date not known to me, but probably soon after his return to Cambridge in 1929) in which he said that he sometimes had a certain experience which could best be described by saying that 'when I have it *I wonder at the existence of the world.* And I am then inclined to use such phrases as "How extraordinary that anything should exist!" or "How extraordinary that the world should exist!"' He went on to say something that is related to the thought expressed in the above-mentioned play: namely, that he sometimes also had 'the experience of feeling *absolutely* safe. I mean the state of mind in which one is inclined to say "I am safe, nothing can injure me *whatever* happens."'

awareness of one's own sin and guilt. He added that he could *not* understand the conception of a *Creator*. I think that the ideas of Divine judgement, forgiveness, and redemption had some intelligibility for him, as being related in his mind to feelings of disgust with himself, an intense desire for purity, and a sense of the helplessness of human beings to make themselves better. But the notion of a being *making the world* had no intelligibility for him at all.

Wittgenstein once suggested that a way in which the notion of immortality can acquire a meaning is through one's feeling that one has duties from which one cannot be released, even by death. Wittgenstein himself possessed a stern sense of duty.

I believe that Wittgenstein was prepared by his own character and experience to comprehend the idea of a judging and redeeming God. But any cosmological conception of a Deity, derived from the notions of cause or of infinity, would be repugnant to him. He was impatient with 'proofs' of the existence of God, and with attempts to give religion a *rational* foundation. When I once quoted to him a remark of Kierkegaard's to this effect: 'How can it be that Christ does not exist, since I know that He has saved me?', Wittgenstein exclaimed: 'You see! It isn't a question of *proving* anything!' He disliked the theological writings of Cardinal Newman, which he read with care during his last year at Cambridge. On the other hand, he revered the writings of St. Augustine. He told me he decided to begin his *Investigations* with a quotation from the latter's *Confessions,* not because he could not find the conception expressed in that quotation stated as well by other philosophers, but because the conception *must* be important if so great a mind held it. Kierkegaard he also esteemed. He referred to him, with something of awe in his expression, as a 'really religious' man. He had read the *Concluding Unscientific Postscript*—but found it 'too deep' for him. The *Journal* of George Fox, the English Quaker, he read with admiration—and presented me with a copy of it. He praised one of Dickens' sketches—an account of the latter's visit on board a passenger ship crowded with English converts to Mormonism, about to sail for America. Wittgenstein was impressed by the calm resolution of those people, as portrayed by Dickens.

I do not wish to give the impression that Wittgenstein accepted any religious faith—he certainly did not—or that he was a religious person. But I think that there was in him, in some sense, the *possibility* of religion. I believe that he looked on religion as a 'form of life' (to use an expression from the *Investigations*) in which he did not participate, but with which he was sympathetic and which greatly interested him. Those who did participate he respected—although here as elsewhere he had contempt for insincerity. I suspect that he regarded religious belief as based on qualities of character and will that he himself did not possess. Of Smythies and Anscombe, both of whom had become Roman Catholics, he once said to me: 'I could not possibly bring myself to believe all the things that they believe.' I think that in this remark he was not disparaging their belief. It was rather an observation about his own capacity.

It was Wittgenstein's character to be deeply pessimistic, both about his own prospects and those of humanity in general. Anyone who was on an intimate footing with Wittgenstein must have been aware of the feeling in him that our lives are ugly and our minds in the dark—a feeling that was often close to despair.

In the summer of 1947 I left Cambridge with my family to return to the States. From America I wrote to Wittgenstein, thanking him for the thoughts that he had so generously imparted to me. He replied:

You know how much I enjoyed being with you at Cambridge. And, of course, you owe me *nothing*. My mind is rather in a turmoil these days. I am almost certain that I shall resign my professorship in the autumn . . . *please keep it to yourself* as it's not yet certain. I *hate* to let down [*here he mentions the name of the man who wished to attend his lectures and whom I had warned, at Wittgenstein's request, of the possibility of his resignation*], but I think I won't be able to help it. I'd like to be alone somewhere & try to write & to make at least one part of my book publishable. I'll never be able to do it while I'm teaching at Cambridge. Also I think that, quite apart from writing, I need a longish spell of thinking *alone*, without having to talk to anybody. But I haven't yet told the authorities about my plan & I don't intend to do so until October when I'll decide definitely.

Three months later (November 1947), after a trip to Austria, he wrote:

As soon as I returned here from Austria, I tendered my resignation to the Vice Chancellor & I shall cease to be professor on Dec. 31st. at 12 p.m. *Whatever* happens to me (& I'm not at all sanguine about my future) I feel I did the only natural thing. I intend to leave here for Ireland in about 3 weeks . . . I'm very busy these days; chiefly, dictating stuff I wrote during the last 2–3 years. It's mostly *bad* but I want to have it with me in a handy form.—I'm seeing Moore once a week. I like being with him almost more than ever. Somehow we seem to understand each other better. He is alternately well & a little ill & has to take it easy.

This letter contained the following postscript:

I had an impertinent letter from [*here again occurs the name of the man to whom I had written at Wittgenstein's request*] reproaching me for not letting him know beforehand about my resignation. He told me that this showed a 'shocking' 'fault of character' & that I was 'a gross person'. I replied & tried to tell him 'where he gets off'. He *seems* to be an ass.

In December Wittgenstein wrote from Red Cross, Wicklow, Eire:

I have only today moved into the above address. It's a little Guest House $2\frac{1}{2}$ to 3 hours by bus from Dublin. It's not *too* bad & I hope I'll acclimatize. I'm the only guest. Of course, right now I still feel completely strange & uncomfortable. That I haven't worked a stroke for ages goes without saying. . . . I wish you lots of luck & I know you wish me the same. Both of us need it like hell. And other people do too.

A month later he wrote to my wife:

This is a pretty quiet place, & if it were still more quiet it would suit me *still* better. My work's going moderately well & I think it might even go very well if I weren't suffering from some kind of indigestion which I don't seem to be able to shake off. I'll have to come to Ithaca & eat your good cooking. . . .

In response to her question as to the wisdom of requiring our eleven-year-old son to sometimes read aloud to us, he added:

I think it's a *very* good idea to make Ray read to you. To practice reading aloud *well*, i.e. carefully, teaches one *a lot*! E.G. how rotten & slapdash most people, & the newspapers, write; & they write as they *think*.

In February 1948, he wrote to me:

I am now in very good bodily health & my work isn't going bad either. I have occasionally queer states of nervous instability about which I'll only say that they're rotten while they last, & teach one to pray.

A Memoir

I had previously written to him about two books—one was Kierkegaard's *The Works of Love,* which greatly impressed me, and the other was Prescott's *Conquest of Peru,* which I had enjoyed. His letter continues:

> I've never read 'The Works of Love'. Kierkegaard is far too deep for me, any how. He bewilders me without working the good effects which he would in *deeper* souls.—Years ago Drury read to Skinner & me the beginning of the 'Conquest of Mexico' which we found very interesting indeed. That I didn't like the parsonish point of view of Prescott's is, of course, a different story.—I am not reading much, thank God. I read in Grimm's fairy tales & in Bismarck's 'Gedanken & Erinnerungen' which I admire greatly. I don't mean, of course, that my views are Bismarck's views. . . . I wish you *lots* of good luck, & I know you wish me the same; & *do I need it*!

He adds as a postscript:

> I haven't anyone at all to talk to here, & this is good & in a way bad. It would be good to see someone occasionally to whom one could say a really friendly word. I don't need *conversations.* What I'd like would be someone to smile at occasionally.

A month later:

> My work is progressing *very* slowly & painfully, but it is progressing. I wish I had more working power & didn't tire so *very* easily. But I have to take it as I find it.

Six weeks later he wrote from a new address, Rosro Cottage, Renvyle P.O., Co. Galway, Eire:

> This is chiefly to give you my new address. I've had a bad time lately: soul, mind & body. I felt exceedingly depressed

for many weeks, then fell ill & now I'm weak & completely dull. I haven't done any work for 5–6 weeks. I'm living alone in a cottage here on the west coast right on the sea, far from civilization. I arrived here 2 days ago & am not yet at home at all. I'll have to learn gradually how to do my housework without losing too much time & strength. . . . What gets me down most is that my nights are bad. If they mend, & I hope they will, I have a chance.

A month later (June 1948) he was in better spirits:

Thanks a lot for the detective mags. I had, before they arrived, been reading a detective story by Dorothy Sayers, & it was so bl . . . foul that it depressed me. Then when I opened one of your mags it was like getting out of a stuffy room into the fresh air. . . . My work's so-so; not too good, not *too* bad. I don't think I'd be much good at philosophical discussion now; but this may mend & then I hope I'll have talks with you!

The next day, having discovered in one of the detective 'mags' a letter from my wife pressing him to visit us in the States, he replied to her as follows:

Thanks a *lot* for inviting me. It's good to know that you won't mind taking me in once the time is ripe. But it isn't now. You see, my main source of trouble is myself &, unfortunately, that would accompany me wherever I go. I'm *much* better now than before I came here. My health is as fine as can be expected of an old codger, & the things that I'm always inclined to beef about are *necessary* evils. My work, e.g. is only so-so; but then my talent is only *that* size & I'm getting a bit shop worn and nothing can help this. I often get exasperated about it but I just must (or *ought* to) learn to bear it. The solitude here is often a strain, but it's also a blessing; that I have to do all my housework is a great strain, but it's undoubtedly a great blessing, too, because it keeps me sane, it *forces* me to live a regular life & is in general good for me *although I curse it every day.* The truth is I oughtn't to be such an old woman & complain such a lot; but then that's also one of the things that can't be changed.—But I hope, *seriously*, to come & stay with you one day when I'll be riper for it. (Of course you know that some apples never get ripe: they're hard & sour until they get soft & mushy.)— The country around here is pretty wild & I enjoy walking in it though I don't go for long walks. I like looking at the various sea birds; we have also seals, though I've only seen one so far. I see nobody except the man who brings me my milk every day. He also helps around the house a little & sees that I don't run out of turf (that's what we heat & cook with). He's quite nice & certainly better company than the people I stayed with in Co Wicklow. The nearest village is 10 miles away. When I want anything special in the way of groceries I write to Galway & they send it here by post.— I hope Fate will let me stay with you some day, & I'm sure I'll enjoy it hugely, I also hope that then I might be useful in discussion (now I'm too stale).

Still at Rosro Cottage in July, he writes to me:

My work isn't going well though it's moving a bit. The other day I asked myself: ought I to have left the University, oughtn't I to have gone on teaching after all? I immediately felt that I couldn't possibly have continued teaching philosophy & even told myself that perhaps I ought to have resigned sooner; but then I thought of you & v. Wright in Cambridge & said to myself that I'd left exactly at the right moment. If my philosophical talent comes to an end now it's bad luck, but that's all.

He announced his intention of remaining at Rosro Cottage for another month and then going to Austria for three or four weeks. Apparently he did go to Austria, and after that spent a fortnight in Cambridge, in October 1948, dictating from his manuscripts. His next letter was written from Ross's Hotel, Parkgate Street, Dublin, in November. He had intended to stop there for only a short time to visit his friend, Drury, and then return to Rosro. But his plans changed:

> When I came here I found to my surprise that I could work again; & as I'm anxious to make hay during the very short period when the sun shines in my brain I've decided not to go to Rosro this winter but to stay here where I've got a warm & quiet room.

When I was in Cambridge in 1946–7 Wittgenstein had loaned me a typescript of the work that was later published as Part I of the *Investigations*, and which I had returned to him before departing for the States. I had just written to ask him whether he could send me a copy of it. To this he replied in the same letter:

> I should *like* you to have a typescript of my stuff but I don't see how I can let you have one at present. There exist only 3 copies. One I have (& I need it), Miss Anscombe has one, Moore has half, or $\frac{3}{4}$ of one & the remaining half or $\frac{1}{4}$ is somewhere among my things in Cambridge. There is no one here who could make another copy from mine, & it would cost a *lot* of money. Of course Miss Anscombe could send you her copy, but, to be quite honest, I'd rather it remained safely in England as long as there are only 3 copies existing. I hope you don't think me beastly. It's nice of you to want a copy of my stuff at all! I'll let you have one as soon as I can get another one made.

As it turned out, when Wittgenstein came to visit us in America he brought the copy that Moore had had, and left it with me upon his return to England. After his death I put it in the hands of his literary executors.

My wife and I occasionally sent small parcels of foodstuffs to Wittgenstein, for which he was always extravagantly grateful. The following is a sample from a letter to my wife:

> Thank you & Norman ever so much for your wonderful present! As I've said before, you should be put under tutelage! And in that case I might try to get 'powers of attorney'. (That's the sort of thing I always read in my detective magazines.) Everything in the box was most useful & grand.

He was still at Ross's Hotel in Dublin, 'working a fair amount & still moderately well. . . . I wish my luck could hold for another six months, for by then I could get a good chunk of work done.'

Four weeks later (January 1949) he reports that his luck did not hold:

> I had a pretty good run of work in the last 3 months, or so, but I fell ill with some sort of infection of the intestines about 3 weeks ago & it hasn't yet cleared up. If it goes on for another week I shall consult a specialist. Of course it hasn't done my work any good. I had to interrupt it completely for a week & after that it just crawled along, as I do when I take a walk these days.

A letter of mine to Wittgenstein at this time contained some comments about Moore. I wrote to Wittgenstein of how I had once told Moore that a well-known philosopher of my acquaintance tended to react with hostility to criticisms of his published philosophical views. Moore seeming to be surprised at this information, I asked him whether he could not understand how professional vanity might make a man resentful of criticism of his writings. Moore, to my astonishment, said

'No!' In relating this to Wittgenstein, I added that this ignorance of human nature was to Moore's credit. Wittgenstein replied:

> Now as to Moore—I don't really understand Moore, &, therefore, what I'll say may be quite wrong. But this is what I'm inclined to say:—That Moore is in some sense extraordinarily childlike is obvious, & the remark you quoted (about vanity) is certainly an example of that childlikeness. There is also a *certain* innocence about Moore; he is, e.g., completely unvain. As to it's being to his '*credit*' to be childlike,—I can't understand that; unless it's also to a *child's* credit. For you aren't talking of the innocence a man has fought for, but of an innocence which comes from a natural absence of a temptation.—I believe that all you wanted to say was that you *liked*, or even *loved*, Moore's childlikeness. And that I can *understand*.—I think that our discrepancy here is not so much one of thoughts as of feelings. I *like* & greatly respect Moore; but that's all. He doesn't warm my heart (or very little), because what warms my heart most is human kindness, & Moore—*just like a child*—is not kind. He is kindly & he can be charming & nice to those he likes & he has great *depth*.—That's how it seems to me. If I'm wrong, I'm wrong.

He goes on to say in the same letter:

> My work is still going fairly well, though not as well as say, 6 weeks ago. That's partly due to the fact that I've been a bit ill, & also that a number of things are greatly worrying me.—Money is not one of them. I am, of course, spending rather a lot, but I'll have enough for another 2 years, I think. During that time, God being willing, I'll get some work done; & that, after all, was why I resigned my professorship. I mustn't worry about money *now*, for if I did I couldn't

work. (What will happen after that time I don't yet know. Maybe I won't live that long anyway.)—One of my present worries is the health of one of my sisters in Vienna. She was operated on [for] cancer a short time ago & the operation, as far as it went, was successful, but she won't have long to live. For that reason I *intend* to go to Vienna sometime next spring; & that's got something to do with you, because if I go & come back to England afterwards I intend to dictate the stuff that I've been writing since last autumn, & *if* I do, I'll send you a copy. May it act as manure on your field.

He did actually bring me a copy of the writings last referred to when he came to the States the following summer. This material is incorporated in Part II of the *Investigations*.

In March 1949, Wittgenstein was still living in Ross's Hotel in Dublin. My wife and I again urged him to visit us in America, to which we received the following reply:

Thank you ever so much for the kind invitation. I got it almost a week ago but I couldn't reply because my thoughts were in such a turmoil; & even today I may not be able to produce anything better than a jumble of incoherent sentences. First let me say (a) that I feel deeply grateful for your kindness & (b) that I feel *strongly* tempted to accept your invitation. But there are huge difficulties.—My eldest sister is, to the best of my knowledge, still alive & my two younger sisters *may* still want me to go to Vienna before long. If this happened I'd probably go to Vienna within the next 3 weeks & stay there for 3 or 4 weeks.—I went to a travel agency to enquire about going to America & found out that the journey there & back would cost me somewhere between 80 & 120 pounds. Further I'm told that you alone will have to pay for my upkeep in America, as I'm not allowed to take with me more than 5 pounds. In fact I gather that you'd have to send affidavits stating that you are able & willing to pay for all my expenses during my stay in the U.S.A. If these regulations did not exist I could, theoretically, spend my own money in America, but in fact *I couldn't afford that.* I could afford the trip only by staying with you for *2 or 3 months* & sponging on you!—Now the prospect of staying with you for that length of time is very pleasant as far as I'm concerned, but there is the snag that I am an elderly man & aging pretty rapidly. I mean, physically, not, as far as I can see, mentally. Now this means that you couldn't take me on any *tours.* I'm all right for strolling about but I can't do *very* much more than I did at Cambridge.—For the same reason I wouldn't be any good at gardening.—If it weren't for all these difficulties I'd come *like a shot*, for I'd love to stay with you, have discussions with one of you & make myself a general nuisance to the other. . . . I imagine that you didn't quite realize all these snags when you invited me. Please take *everything* that I've said in this letter seriously & at it's face-value.

I sent Wittgenstein the required affidavit and reassured him on the other points. In his next letter he announces that he has booked an ocean passage. He adds:

In this life one doesn't know what's going to happen; & so, supposing later on you were inclined, *for whatever reason,* to change your mind about the desirability of my visit, please *don't hesitate* to tell me so. . . . I haven't been doing any work at all for the last 2–3 weeks. My mind is tired & stale, partly I think because I'm a bit exhausted, partly because lots of things worry me terribly just now. I think I could still discuss philosophy if I had someone here to discuss with, but alone I can't concentrate on it. I suppose it'll all change again some day. The sooner the better.—Well, then, please send me that affidavit & prepare yourself for the shock of seeing me.

In May he writes from Dublin:

I went to Vienna in the middle of April to see my eldest sister who is very ill. When I left 5 days ago she was still alive but there is no hope of her recovery. I arrived here last night. While I was in Vienna I was hardly able to write at all. I felt so rotten myself. I haven't done any work since the beginning of March & I haven't had the strength of even *trying* to do any. God knows how things will go on now. . . . I hope all of you are well, & I hope you won't find me a terribly disagreeable companion & bore when I come.

In June, still at Dublin:

When I arrived here 3 weeks ago I went to see my doctor & he had my blood examined. They found that I had a severe anaemia of a rather unusual kind. It was suspected that I had a growth in my stomach but the x-ray definitely showed that there is no such thing inside me. I'm being given a lot of iron & liver extract & am getting better slowly. I think I shall certainly be able to sail with the Queen Mary on July 21st. There is, however, the question how far my anaemia will affect my ability to discuss. At present I am quite unable to do any philosophy & I don't think I'd be strong enough to have even a moderately decent discussion. In fact at present I'm *sure* I couldn't do it. But of course it's possible that by the end of July I may have recovered sufficiently for my brain to work again. . . . I *know* that you'd extend your hospitality to me even if I were *completely* dull & stupid, but *I* wouldn't want to be a mere dead weight in your house. I want to feel that I can at least give *a little* for so much kindness.

When I suggested that he need not think of paying for his visit with philosophy he answered:

I never meant to *pay* for your kindness in discussions. Anyhow, the best I could give you would be lousy payment. All I meant was: I don't want to bore my kind hosts to *death*. However, let's not talk about it anymore, especially as I've got good news: I've improved greatly during the last few days. So, obviously, the iron & liver extract do work.

He went on to say that if I should not be able to meet him in New York he would 'jolly well' make the eight- or nine-hour train trip to Ithaca alone. 'Maybe, like in the films, I'll find a beautiful girl whom I meet on the boat & who will help me.'

I went to New York to meet Wittgenstein at the ship. When I first saw him I was surprised at his apparent physical vigour. He was striding down the ramp with a pack on his back, a heavy suitcase in one hand, cane in the other. He was in very good spirits and not at all exhausted and he would not allow me to help him with his luggage. My chief recollection of the long train ride home is that we talked about music and that he whistled for me, with striking accuracy and expressiveness, some parts of Beethoven's 7th Symphony.

During the first month or six weeks that he lived with us his health was fairly good. He loved to go for walks in some nearby woods, with either my wife or myself. His stamina was surprising. On those walks he took a great interest in identifying the kinds of trees. One walk I remember particularly well. Wittgenstein wanted to determine the heights of the trees. Our procedure, invented by him, was that Wittgenstein would place himself at a sufficient distance from the tree to be measured, so that when he sighted along his arm and cane at the top of the tree, his arm was at an angle of roughly 45 degrees from the horizontal. I would pace off the distance from him to the foot of the tree, and a simple calculation gave us its approximate height. Wittgenstein directed this activity with real zest.

My wife once gave him some Swiss cheese and rye bread for lunch, which he greatly liked. Thereafter he would more or less insist on eating bread and cheese at all meals, largely ignoring the various dishes that my wife prepared. Wittgenstein declared that it did not much matter to him *what* he ate, so long as it was always the *same*. When a dish that looked especially appetizing was brought to the table, I sometimes exclaimed 'Hot Ziggety!'—a slang phrase that I learned as a boy in Kansas. Wittgenstein picked up this expression from me. It was inconceivably droll to hear him exclaim 'Hot Ziggety!' when my wife put the bread and cheese before him. During the first part of his visit Wittgenstein insisted on helping to wash the dishes after meals, and he was as before very fussy about the amount of soap and hot water that ought to be used and whether there was the right sort of dish mop. Once he rebuked me sternly for not rinsing properly. Before long, however, he left the dishes alone, and indeed his bodily strength so declined that he was not equal to that exertion.

One of Wittgenstein's favourite phrases was the exclamation, 'Leave the *bloody* thing *alone!*' He delivered this with a most emphatic intonation and mock solemnity of expression. It had roughly the signification that the thing in question was adequate and one should not try to improve it. He used it on a variety of occasions: one time meaning that the location of his bed was satisfactory and it should not be moved; another time, that the mending that my wife had done on a jacket of his was sufficient and that she should not try to make it better.

When the float in the toilet tank once failed to function, Wittgenstein took a lively interest in helping me to repair it. He had an obvious relish for a mechanical problem. When the repair was made, but I proposed adding one more adjustment, Wittgenstein stopped me with the words, 'Leave the *bloody* thing *alone*!' At Trinity College, Wittgenstein had taken me to look at one of the toilets in order to inspect its sturdy construction, and now he commented unfavourably on the construction of ours. He always had a keen appreciation of sound workmanship and a genuinely moral disapproval of the flimsy or the slip-shod. He liked to think that there might be craftsmen who would insist on doing their jobs to *perfection*, and for no reason other than that that was the way it *ought* to be.

Soon after his arrival Wittgenstein proposed that he and I should read his book together. This we did for a few meetings, but again I found that activity too confining and not a satisfactory way of doing philosophy together; and I believe that Wittgenstein came to feel the same. He had numerous philosophical discussions that summer with various persons. With Oets Bouwsma and me he began to read Frege's paper 'Über Sinn und Bedeutung'; and this led to two or three meetings in which Wittgenstein expounded his divergence from Frege. Then in one meeting we discussed free will and determinism. With Willis Doney and me he began to read the *Tractatus*, but this was not kept up. One anecdote should be recorded. I asked Wittgenstein whether, when he wrote the *Tractatus*, he had ever decided upon anything as an *example* of a 'simple object'. His reply was that at that time his thought had been that he was a *logician*; and that it was not his business, as a logician, to try to decide whether this thing or that was a simple thing or a complex thing, that being a purely *empirical* matter! It was clear that he regarded his former opinion as absurd.

With John Nelson, Doney, and myself, Wittgenstein met once to discuss a problem about memory. He met several times for discussions on various topics with some of my Cornell colleagues, among them Max Black and Stuart Brown,

Bouwsma and myself also being present. In some of these meetings Wittgenstein showed the fire and vigour that was characteristic of him in Cambridge. Illness eventually stopped his attendance. At the beginning of the autumn term he met on two consecutive evenings with the Cornell graduate students of philosophy, once talking about verification, once about knowledge.

But the discussions that were of most value to me that summer were a series that took place between Wittgenstein and me, our topic being Moore's 'Proof of An External World' and also his 'Defence of Common Sense'. In particular, we talked about Moore's insistence that it is a correct use of language for him to say, when holding one of his hands before him, 'I *know* that this is a hand'; or to say, while pointing at a tree a few feet away, 'I *know* for *certain* that this is a *tree!*' In a published article I had maintained that this was a senseless use of 'know', and Moore had made a spirited reply to me in a letter. Wittgenstein and I discussed these matters in a number of conversations, he making many observations of the first importance about the concept of knowledge. The following is a brief account of them, based on rough notes that I made:

There is a tendency to think of knowledge as a *mental state*. Now I am supposed to know my own mental states. If I say I have a certain mental state and do not have it, then I have told a lie. But I can say that I know so & so, and it can turn out that so & so is false; but it doesn't follow that I lied. Therefore, knowing is not a mental state.

Mental states, such as anxiety and pain, have degrees. *Certainty* also has degrees, e.g. 'How certain are you?' Since certainty has degrees we are helped to have the idea that knowledge is a mental state.

Moore would like to stare at a house that is only 20 feet

away and say, with a peculiar intonation, 'I *know* that *there's* a *house*!' He does this because he wants to produce in himself the *feeling* of knowing. He wants to exhibit *knowing for certain* to himself. In this way he has the idea that he is replying to the sceptical philosopher who claims that everyday examples of knowing that there is a dog in the backyard, or that the neighbour's house is on fire, are not really or strictly *knowledge*, are not knowledge *in the highest degree*. It is as if someone had said 'You don't really feel pain when you are pinched' and Moore then pinched himself in order to feel the pain, and thus prove to himself that the other is wrong. Moore treats the sentence 'I know so & so' like the sentence 'I have a pain.' The criterion that he knows that so & so will be that he *says* that he does.

Physical-object statements, like 'That's a tree,' sometimes play a role similar to that of mathematical propositions, in the respect that experience could not refute them. If I walked over to that tree and could touch nothing I might lose confidence in everything my senses told me, just as I might lose confidence in all calculations if some simple addition kept coming out differently. Moore said 'I *know* that there's a tree,' partly because of the feeling that if it turned out *not* to be a tree, he would have to 'give up'.

I might refuse to regard anything as *evidence* that there isn't a tree. If I were to walk over to it and to feel nothing at all, I might say that I was *then* deluded, not that I was previously mistaken in thinking it a tree. If I say that I would not *call* anything 'evidence' against that's being a tree, then I am not making a psychological prediction—but a *logical* statement.

In the ordinary use of 'know' it is always sensible to speak of 'making sure'. Now Moore says, e.g. 'I know that this is a shoe' in circumstances where it doesn't have any sense to 'make sure'. And this may actually be a reason for his insistence on saying 'I know' in this case. He may be wishing to say that there can't be any such thing as a further 'making sure' that this is a shoe; and that if there could be a further 'making sure' what better would it give me than what I now have. We have to come to a stop! If there is a making sure *here*, then there is no making sure at all! Moore's statement 'I *know* that this is a shoe' may amount to saying: 'There isn't any *making sure* that this is a shoe; and no matter what might happen I shouldn't call it evidence against this being a shoe.

Instead of saying that Moore's statement 'I know that this is a tree' is a misuse of language, it is better to say that it has no clear meaning, and that Moore himself doesn't know how he is using it. We can *suspect* that he is using it to make some philosophical point, e.g. that some physical-object statements function like mathematical statements; or the point that it is a misusage of language to say 'Perhaps it is not a tree.' But Moore himself isn't clear what he means by it. It isn't even clear to him that he is not giving it an ordinary usage. He is confused by the difference between using it in some ordinary sense and using it to make a philosophical point.

At this stage of our discussion Wittgenstein came to the conclusion that, contrary to what he had previously said, it is *false* that 'In the ordinary use of "know" it is always sensible to speak of "making sure"':

There is an ordinary use of 'I know' when there isn't any *making sure*. E.g. a sighted person could say it to a blind man who asks 'Are you sure that it's a tree?' And also when we have *completed* an investigation we can say, 'I know now that it's a tree.' Another example: if you and I were coming through woods toward a house and I broke out into the clearing and there was the house right before me, I might exclaim 'There's the house.' You, back in the bushes, might ask doubtfully 'Are you sure?', and I should reply 'I *know* it.' Here the use of 'I know it' would be natural, and yet it would also be a case of certainty 'in the highest degree', a case in which I should be willing to count nothing as evidence that there isn't a house there.

Moore might have given such examples, examples of a use of 'I know' in which that expression really functions 'im sprachlichen Verkehr' i.e. in the actual traffic of language, in 'the stream of life'. But he doesn't give such examples: he prefers to gaze at a tree and say 'I *know* there's a tree there. And this is because he wants to give himself the *experience* of knowing.

We might say 'A human being knows that he has two hands' and mean by this, that he doesn't have to count them or make sure that there are still two—whereas some other creatures might have hands that occasionally disappeared.

'The earth has existed for one million years' has sense; 'The earth has existed for five minutes' is nonsense. What if someone argued that the latter has sense because it is *implied* by the former?

Are not some of Moore's 'truisms' more absurd than others? It isn't difficult to think of usages for 'I know that this is a hand'; it is more difficult for 'I know that the earth has existed for many years'; it is still more difficult for 'I know that I am a human being.' To understand a sentence is to be prepared for one of its uses. If we can't think of any use for it at all, then we don't understand it at all.

Experiential propositions do not all have the same logical status. With regard to some, of which we say that we *know* them to be true, we can imagine circumstances on the basis of which we should say that the statement had turned out to be false. But with others there are no circumstances in which we should say 'it turned out to be false'. This is a logical remark and has nothing to do with what I shall say 10 minutes from now.

Moore's propositions—'I know that I am a human being,' 'I know that the earth has existed for many years,' etc.— have this characteristic, that it is impossible to think of circumstances in which we should allow that we have evidence against them. But when the sceptical philosophers say 'You don't know' and Moore replies 'I do know,' his reply is quite useless, unless it is to assure them that he, Moore, doesn't feel any doubt whatever. But that is not what is at issue.

These philosophers want to make a *logical* point. They want to say we don't know something to be true if future experience can disprove it. There are kinds of statements that future experience cannot refute, e.g. sense-datum statements, and mathematical or logical statements. To use 'I know' with sense-datum statements is silly. It adds nothing. In mathematics it isn't silly. And there is a close resemblance between some experiential statements and mathematical ones— namely, future experience won't provide reasons for rejecting them.

The sceptical philosophers want to say that with experiential statements, 'I know it' is the the same as 'I believe it and it is true.' They think that degree of *certainty* is degree of *conviction*. They interpret Moore's 'I know it with absolute certainty' as an expression of extreme conviction. What is needed is to show them that the highest degree of certainty is nothing psychological but something logical: that there is a point at which there is neither any 'making more certain' nor any 'turning out to be false'. Some experiential statements have this property. Some others are related in various ways to those that have this property. Thus we can give a logical justification of the use of 'I know' with experiential statements.

In teaching words to a child one does not say either 'I *believe* that that is red' or 'I *know* that that is red,' but simply 'That is red.' If one's teaching was always expressed with *doubt*, it is difficult to say whether the child would learn anything. He certainly would not learn to express himself *with reservations*. Unless words like 'red' and 'chair' are learned there isn't any language.

Proofs in mathematics involve the writing of equations on paper and seeing that one expression is contained in another. But if it is always to be doubted what expressions appear on a paper, then there can't be any proofs or any mathematics.

It could happen sometimes that my senses deceived me, but not all the time. Hallucinations must be the exception. Mistakes in mathematics must be the exception. A physical-object judgement turning out to be false must be the exception.

Moore's attempt to find a difference in his experience between 'knowing' and 'being certain' is like this: that I should say that I see something different when I see Wittgenstein in a mirror from what I see when I see *myself* in a mirror.

Certain propositions belong to my 'frame of reference'. If I had to give *them* up, I shouldn't be able to judge *anything*. Take the example of the earth's having existed for many years before I was born. What evidence against it could there be? A document?

Doubt, belief, certainty—like feelings, emotions, pain, etc. —have characteristic facial expressions. Knowledge does *not* have a characteristic facial expression. There is a *tone* of doubt, and a tone of conviction, but no tone of knowledge.

The foregoing notes are not intended to be verbatim, although some phrases and sentences actually are verbatim. The notes were written up a day or two after each talk. They are a condensed summary of what I took away from a number of discussions, occurring over a period of several weeks. A few of the thoughts may have been my own, but certainly most were not. I believe that these notes give a reasonably accurate report of part, although certainly not all, that Wittgenstein said. Nonetheless I wish to issue an emphatic warning that they do not pretend to give an authentic version of his thoughts. One remark of his struck me then, as it does now, as being especially noteworthy and as summing up a good deal of his philosophy. It is 'Ein Ausdruck hat nur im Strome des Lebens Bedeutung' (An expression has meaning only in the stream of life). Wittgenstein believed that this aphorism was written down in one of his manuscripts; and perhaps it is, but not in any that I have seen.

On one of our walks Wittgenstein said that if he had the money he thought he would have his book (Part I of the *Investigations*) mimeographed and distributed among his friends. He said that it was not in a completely finished state, but that he did not think that he could give the final polish to it in his lifetime. This plan would have the merit that he could put in parentheses after a remark, expressions of dissatisfaction, like 'This is not quite right' or 'This is fishy.' He would like to put his book into the hands of his friends, but to take it to a publisher right then was out of the question. He asked me what I thought of this idea of mimeographing it. I replied that I did not like it at all. Wittgenstein was angered by my remark. He suggested that, like other students of his, I was reluctant to see his work made public because people would then know where my own philosophical ideas came from. What I had felt was not what he supposed, but rather that it was not fitting that a book of that importance should be distributed in mimeograph: instead it should be bound in 'leather and gold'.

More than once, Wittgenstein said to me that it was a

problem for him as to what to do with the remainder of his life. 'When a person has only one thing in the world—namely, a certain talent—what is he to do when he begins to lose that talent?' he asked. Wittgenstein spoke so earnestly and sombrely that I, knowing that three of his brothers had committed suicide, feared that he might attempt the same.

The weather was unusually hot that summer and Wittgenstein's room on the second floor was often very uncomfortable. He once pointed out to me that the wire mesh of the window screens restricted to some extent the movement of air through his windows, and wondered why they could not be removed. I replied that if this were done great numbers of insects would enter and prove even more disagreeable than the heat. Wittgenstein doubted that this was so. He remarked that in England and on the Continent windows were commonly left unscreened. I answered that there were more insects in America. Wittgenstein didn't believe this, and when he went out for a walk later that day he made a point of looking at a number of houses in order to see whether their windows were screened. He found that all of them were but, oddly enough, instead of inferring that there must be a good reason for it, he concluded with some irritation that Americans were the victims of widespread and unthinking prejudice as to the necessity of window screens!

Wittgenstein became extremely ill during the latter part of his stay with us. He had a painful bursitis in both shoulders, was unable to sleep, and was extremely weak. His doctor arranged for him to spend two days in the hospital to obtain a complete physical examination. On the day before he went to the hospital he was not only ill, but also frightened. He had told me previously that his father died of cancer and, in addition, his favourite sister was gradually dying of the same disease, despite several operations. Wittgenstein's fear was not that he would be found to have cancer (he was quite prepared for that) but that he might be kept at the hospital for surgery. His fear of surgery came near to panic. It was not the operation itself he dreaded, but to become a useless and bed-ridden invalid whose death had only been deferred for a little. He was also very afraid that the doctors might prevent him from making the return passage to England in October, which was already booked. 'I don't want to die in America. I am a European—I want to die in Europe,' he murmured to me in a frenzy. And he exclaimed: 'What a fool I was to come.'

He returned from the hospital in quite a cheerful frame of mind. The examination had not found anything seriously wrong with him (although later that autumn he was discovered to have cancer); and there was no longer any threat of his being detained in the hospital or of his departure for England being postponed. I did not see how he could make the trip since he was so extremely weak: but in the two weeks before he sailed he recovered strength in a surprising way.

Wittgenstein returned to England in October. Early in December I received the following letter from Cambridge:

> The doctors have now made their diagnosis. I have cancer of the prostate. But this sounds, in a way, much worse than it is, for there is a drug (actually some hormones) which can, as I'm told, alleviate the symptoms of the disease so that I can live on for years. The doctor even tells me that I may be able to work again, but I can't imagine that. I was in no way shocked when I heard I had cancer, but I *was* when I heard that one could do something about it, because I had *no* wish to live on. But I couldn't have my wish. I am treated with great kindness by everyone & I have an immensely kind doctor who isn't a fool either.

A few days later he asked me to 'not *under any circumstances* let *any* one know about the nature of my illness who doesn't already know about it. . . . This is of the greatest importance for me as I plan to go to Vienna for Christmas & *not* to let my family know about the real disease.'

Wittgenstein went to Vienna in December, and remained until the end of March. A letter in January says that he is very well and not at all depressed. He remarks how extremely lucky he was that his illness was not correctly diagnosed in America. He adds:

> My brain works very sluggishly these days but I can't say I mind. I'm reading various odds & ends, e.g. Goethe's Theory of colour which, with all its absurdities, has very interesting points, & stimulates me to think. . . . I'm not writing at all because my thoughts never sufficiently crystallize. Not that it matters.

In April 1950 he was back in England. He had received an invitation to give the John Locke lectures in Oxford, for which he would receive two hundred pounds. But there would be an audience of 200 and the lectures would have to be quite formal and there could be no discussion. He declined this invitation and the reason he gave to me was, 'I don't think I can give formal lectures to a large audience that would be any good.' That spring I succeeded in interesting a director of the Rockefeller Foundation, Chadbourne Gilpatric, in the possibility of awarding Wittgenstein a research grant. I informed Wittgenstein of this and, after thanking me for undertaking it, he replied:

> The thought of being able to live where I like, of not having to be a burden or a nuisance to others, of doing philosophy when my nature inclines me to do it is, of course, pleasant for me, as it would be for anyone else who wants to do philosophy. But I could not accept money from the Rockefeller Foundation unless the directors knew the com-

plete truth about me. The truth is this. (a) I have not been able to do any sustained good work since the beginning of March, 1949. (b) Even before that date I could not work *well* for more than 6 or 7 months a year. (c) As I'm getting older my thoughts become markedly less forceful & crystallize more rarely & I get tired very much more easily. (d) My health is in a somewhat labile state owing to a constant slight anaemia which inclines me to catch infections. This further diminishes the chance of my doing really good work. (e) Though it's impossible for me to make any definite predictions, it seems to me likely that my mind will never again work as vigorously as it did, say, 14 months ago. (f) I cannot promise to publish anything during my lifetime.

I believe that as long as I live & as often as the state of my mind permits it I will think about philosophical problems & try to write about them. I also believe that much of what I wrote in the past 15 or 20 years may be of interest to people when it's published. But it is, nevertheless, perfectly possible that *all* that I'm *going* to produce will be flat, uninspired & uninteresting. There are many examples of people who did excellent work when they were young, & *very* dull work indeed when they got old.

I think this is all I can say about it. I believe you should show this letter to the director you approached about me. It is obviously impossible to accept a grant under false pretences, and you *may*, unintentionally, have presented my case in too rosy a light.

During part of 1950, Wittgenstein lived in Oxford in Anscombe's home. In July he wrote: 'I have hardly any philosophical discussions. I could see students if I wanted, but I don't want to. I've got all sorts of unclear thoughts in my old head which perhaps will remain there forever in this unsatisfactory state.' Oets Bouwsma and his family spent that year in

Oxford. Wittgenstein used to visit them and loved eating Mrs. Bouwsma's home-made apple-sauce. In a letter to me he remarked of his inability to do philosophical work, 'I am just good enough to eat apple-sauce with a philosopher.'

In the autumn of 1950, Wittgenstein went to Norway for five weeks with a companion who fell ill twice with bronchitis during that period:

> So there was no end of trouble. . . . I had intended to do some work but I didn't do any. I may possibly go back to Norway before long & try to work. It's the only place I know where I can have real quiet. Of course it's possible that I'm no longer able to do any decent research, but it's certainly worth while finding out if I am or not.

Wittgenstein later wrote that he had arranged to spend the winter on the farm of a friend in Norway and had booked a passage for December 30th but had to cancel the trip because of illness. In January of 1951 he writes that Gilpatric of the Rockefeller Foundation has been to visit him. 'I told him what I wrote to you some months ago, i.e. that in my present state of health & intellectual dullness I couldn't accept a grant; but I said that if, against all probability & hope, I should one day find that I could again do worthwhile work in philosophy, I'd write to him. And so we parted on friendly terms.' He goes on to say that Oxford 'is a philosophical desert'. (It was reported to me that Wittgenstein had also referred to the philosophical circles of Oxford as 'the influenza area', a remark that gave offence to some Oxford dons.) He adds: 'My mind's completely dead. This isn't a complaint, for I don't really suffer from it. I know that life must have an end once & that mental life can cease before the rest does.'

Soon after this he went to Cambridge to stay in the home of his physician, Dr. Bevan. (When Wittgenstein first learned from Dr. Bevan that he had cancer, he expressed an extreme aversion and even fear of spending his last days in a hospital. Dr. Bevan then told him that he could come to his house to die. Wittgenstein was deeply grateful for this human offer.) He had previously been very ill in Oxford, but was now better, although still not well. 'I can't even *think* of work at present, & it doesn't matter, if only I don't live too long! I'm not depressed though.' He remained at Dr. Bevan's until his death. In March he writes that he is feeling much better and suffering hardly any pain. 'I am of course very weak & there seems no doubt that this isn't going to change for the better as time goes on. I hardly think that I'll be on this earth when you come to Cambridge in Autumn '52. Still, one doesn't know. I am not depressed in the least, by the way.' Two months previously he had sent me the biography of Rommel by Brigadier Young. In this same letter he remarks 'I'm very glad you liked the Rommel book. I looked at it quite recently again & was impressed again by the thoroughly *decent* way in which it's written. Such books are few & far between.'

The last letter that I received from Wittgenstein was written 13 days before his death. He says: 'An extraordinary thing happened to me. About a month ago I suddenly found myself in the right frame of mind for doing philosophy. I had been *absolutely* certain that I'd never again be able to do it. It's the first time after more than 2 years that the curtain in my brain has gone up.—Of course, so far I've only worked for about 5 weeks & it may be all over by tomorrow; but it bucks me up a lot now.' He also says that 'apart from a certain weakness which has constant ups & downs I'm feeling *very* well these days'.

When Wittgenstein came to live with the Bevans, Mrs. Bevan was at first frightened of him, but soon became devoted. They took many walks together. As she told me, his influence over her came to be great, even in little things. For example, she had bought a new coat to wear to a party, and before leaving the house, went to show it to Wittgenstein. He scrutinized it carefully, said 'Wait!' in a peremptory tone, took a pair of scissors and, without asking permission, cut several large buttons off the front. And she liked the coat better that way!

Wittgenstein was feeling extremely well and working furiously. At the time when 'the curtain went up' he said to Mrs. Bevan: 'I am going to work now as I have never worked before!'

On Friday, April 27th, he took a walk in the afternoon. That night he fell violently ill. He remained conscious and when informed by the doctor that he could live only a few days, he exclaimed 'Good!' Before losing consciousness he said to Mrs. Bevan (who was with him throughout the night) 'Tell them I've had a wonderful life!' By 'them' he undoubtedly meant his close friends. When I think of his profound pessimism, the intensity of his mental and moral suffering, the relentless way in which he drove his intellect, his need for love together with the harshness that repelled love, I am inclined to believe that his life was fiercely unhappy. Yet at the end he himself exclaimed that it had been 'wonderful'! To me this seems a mysterious and strangely moving utterance.